Edith Stein Discovered

Edith Stein on the threshold of Cologne Carmel
enclosure door, 1938

Edith Stein Discovered:
A Personal Portrait

Pat Lyne OCDS

Templegate Publishers
Springfield, Illinois

First published in England in 2000
Gracewing
2 Southern Avenue, Leominster
Herefordshire HR6 0QF

First published in the United States in 2001

Templegate Publishers
302 East Adams Street
Post Office Box 5152
Springfield, Illinois
62705-5152
217-522-3353
templegate.com

Copyright © 2000 Pat Lyne

ISBN 0-87243-252-1
Library of Congress Control Number:
2001 131577

Contents

List of Illustrations

(iv) Edith and Rosa at Echt, July 1939.
8(i) Station Master Fouquet.
(ii) The memorial plaque at Schifferstadt station.

Copyright Acknowledgements

A Note on Quotations

Quotations from, and references to, the autobiography, correspondence and essays of Edith Stein are taken from the following editions (American spelling has been modified for publication in England):

Life in a Jewish Family. Her Unfinished Autobiographical Account [1891–1916], tr. Josephine Koeppel, OCD, eds. Dr L Gelber and Romaeus Leuven, OCD, Washington: ICS Publications (The Collected Works of Edith Stein, vol. 1), 1986.

Self-Portrait in Letters 1916–1942, tr. Josephine Koeppel, OCD, eds. Dr L Gelber and Romaeus Leuven, OCD, Washington: ICS Publications (The Collected Works of Edith Stein, vol. 5), 1993.

The Hidden Life. Hagiographic Essays, Meditations, Spiritual Texts, tr. Waltraut Stein, eds. Dr L Gelber and Romaeus Leuven, OCD, Washington: ICS Publications (The Collected Works of Edith Stein, vol. 4), 1992.

Essays on Woman, tr. Freda Mary Oben, eds. Dr L Gelber and Romaeus Leuven, OCD, Washington: ICS Publications (The Collected Works of Edith Stein, vol. 2), 2nd ed. revised, 1996.

Sources for other quotations are indicated in footnotes. The full reference is given on the first occurrence.

For a list of the main secondary sources on Edith Stein which have been consulted for this book, see the Select Bibliography.

Preface

In the early 1980s, I was in the process of a big change in my life. It was a difficult time as I tried to adapt and I found myself in need of a friend who might understand. I found that friend in Edith Stein. *Life in a Jewish Family* became my daily companion and I walked beside Edith as her memories rose to the surface. In order to know her better, I read biographies, studies, and such of her own works as were available in English. I visited Cologne Carmel on three separate occasions. I prayed in Beuron Abbey and I met those closely associated with work concerning her life: Sister Amata, her archivist, Sister Josephine Koeppel, her translator, and Father John Sullivan OCD, a loyal supporter of her Cause. Edith became my inspiration and I felt a strong bond growing between us. In the year of her canonisation, I decided to share this bond with others by writing a personal portrait. I have felt Edith's guidance and support at my right hand throughout my task. It was through her that I met Joanne Mosley who has acted as translator, sympathetic editor and everlasting moral support. In addition, she enlisted her mother's assistance as painstaking typist of the manuscript. I can never thank them both enough.

I am deeply grateful to all those who have responded to my request for photographs and their permission to use them, as well as books and other information. They are: Sr Josephine Koeppel, OCD (Elysburg, Pennsylvania); Sr Amata Neyer, OCD (Cologne); Sr Marie-Thérèse Konieczna, OP (Speyer); Sr

Maria Brüning, OSU (Dorsten); Beek Carmel; Laura Meaux, O Carm Secular (Monheim); Hubert Vögele (Ilvesheim); Frau Irmgard Dobler, Edith-Stein-Gesellschaft Deutschland (Speyer); and my good friends Edith and Beatrice Milleder (Munich).

I hope that this short biography will encourage many more people to appreciate Edith Stein as the 'Saint for our Times',[1] a ray of pure light in the darker moments of our times.

---

[1] From the title of the biography by Sr Amata Neyer; see Select Bibliography.

Foreword

As a child Edith Stein had an intimation that she would be great. Her professor Husserl realized that 'in her everything is absolutely true'. It is this passion for truth that marks the whole trajectory of her life and accounts for both her intense dedication to the pursuit of knowledge and the evolution of her spiritual life from a love of science to prayer, to the cloister and finally the witness that brought her to Auschwitz. In her case the monstrous tragedy of the Holocaust had a different kind of solution: 'the wood of the cross has become the light of Christ'. That kindly light led her, even when she was entirely unaware of her 'happy lot'. Her quest for truth took on a new sense of urgency when she read St Teresa's *Life* at a sitting and concluded: '*das ist die Wahrheit*' ('that is the Truth'). From then on she realized that 'it is always an adventure to respond to the call of God, but God is worth the risk'. For Edith that call implied the paradox of exclusiveness, something to which she clung through years of teaching and lecturing until the political situation closed that way to her and she was welcomed at the Carmel of Cologne. Edith was a professional philosopher and it is greatly to the credit of the Carmelites that they gave her scope to continue her research, even if it was made more arduous by the circumstances of time and place. Because Edith had become a Christian and because of her demands of faith on her thinking, her philosophy could no longer ignore theology. For her, God speaks to the intelligence by his word. Intellectual understanding became a spiritual search, the end of which was the living God, the means a purification of heart and spirit. Her intellectual work is necessarily truncated; even her autobiographical writing was rudely interrupted by the SS knock on the door of Echt Carmel to which she and Rosa had gone to escape the terror. But we have enough to converse with one of the great women of our time.

In this lucidly written book, Pat Lyne provides us with an engaging portrait of a saint with whom we feel she has such affinity. Her familiarity with her personal writings and her knowledge of the places associated with Edith give it a ring of authenticity. I think that her judgement is reliable about Edith, the person and her relationships. In fact, I never find myself disagreeing with her when she undertakes an independent opinion. It is important to meet the woman who became a philosopher and eventually a saint before grappling with her thought and the author's book seems to me to be the perfect introduction. Edith herself placed the person before the intellectual reflex.

Nicholas Madden OCD
Feast of St Elijah 1999

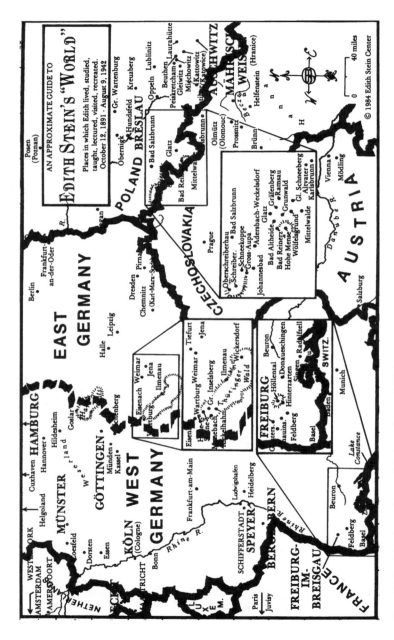

Note: National borders reflect political entities as of 1984.

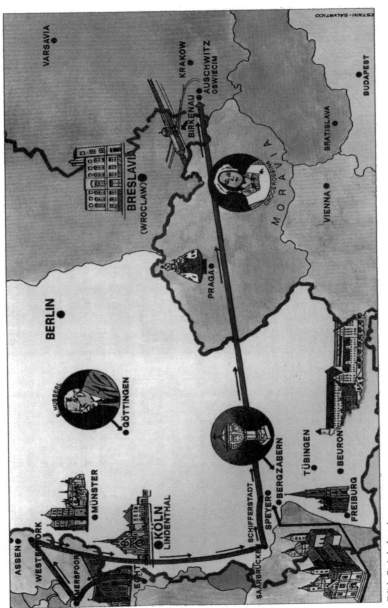

Edith Stein's last journey

CHAPTER ONE

Breslau is Home

Edith wrote the first chapter of her *Life in a Jewish Family* in 1933 during her last weeks at home in Breslau. She was forty-two years old and her mother's youngest and favourite child. Mother and daughter knew that a final parting was not far off. It was a time of inner anguish but also one of close companionship.

Auguste Stein sat down in the evenings with her knitting and shared the pros and cons of her day's work at the timber yard. Edith had always taken a keen interest in such things, knowing how dear they were to her mother's heart. The conversation moved on to the old lady's memories of her youth and the lifestyle of her family, the Courants, as she remembered it. Edith learnt how her great-grandparents had lived and met and married and reared their families. How the Steins and the Courants had come together and how the strong bonds engendered in these large Jewish families had been handed from one generation to the next. What precious evenings these were for both mother and daughter.

When they retired for the night, it is likely Edith sat at her old desk, where so many hours of study had been spent in the past, in order to record her mother's memories. She gave Chapter I the title 'My Mother Remembers 1815–1891'. It was written in Latin script on foolscap paper, largely on one side only, for it was 'scrap' paper, corrected sheets from students' notebooks or carbon copies of her own work on St Thomas Aquinas.

It is apparent from her Foreword that Edith's original intention was not to write her own story, an autobiography, but, as the title says, to portray life in a Jewish family. At the same time, it was important to Edith that her mother, who was pivotal to the life of the Stein family, should have her memories and life proclaimed faithfully. And this she did. Perhaps it is inevitable that once Edith left home to pursue her career in Göttingen in 1913, the story does at last become 'hers'.

Auguste Stein was a matriarchal figure whose immense strength of character and justice guided the family through the daily trials and joys of life. She was a lady of formidable powers who could run a timber business and a large family; who could find time to practise her Jewish faith in all its fullness; who never omitted to show charity to her large extended family in their many troubles, and who treated those who worked for her with fairness and consideration, well beyond the normal call of duty. From this we should not deduce that Auguste was a hard woman or one who dominated her children. Edith always had total freedom in the choices she made throughout her life. Favourite child she may have been but tied to her mother's apron-strings she never was. While thrift was necessary in the running of the household, there was no poverty. All members of the family were content to live confidently dependent on their mother's providence and never permitted themselves to contemplate a time without her. Throughout her life, Edith remembered her mother's hands as being warm, however cold it might be outside. For her, this symbolized how the warmth of the Stein household stemmed from her. As a tiny child, she jumped into the arms of her mother on her return from work and the hands which grasped her were always warm. This, then, was the mother who had such a profound influence on Edith and from whom she inherited many of her sterling qualities. While they were very close, her mother was not her confidante. At that time there was no such person in her life. Nonetheless, she writes: 'our destinies are intertwined in such a unique way, it is probably appropriate that in this portrait of my mother I say more about my own development than about that of my brothers or sisters.'

As the story unfolds in Chapters II and III, 'The World as the Two Youngest Knew It' and 'Care and Dissension in the

Family', readers may find the minutiae of family life all too familiar. The ups and downs are reminiscent of many another family and on occasion, Edith finds herself 'anticipating' her own story while following that of her older brothers and sisters. We must remember this was written after she had entered Carmel and before her first profession. They were her personal memories recalled in a monastic atmosphere far from family and home. She appears to write as 'occasions' stir her memory and there is a certain lack of orderliness – strange when you are aware Edith was the most orderly of people.

The spontaneous script provides an honest and clear portrait of the numerous relatives and friends included in the story, and the many anecdotal asides are jewels in themselves. You discover how often it is Edith who is able to provide the healing 'note', or sound advice in the family conflicts. You learn how from her teenage years that she had a 'way' with children, nursing them when sick, reading them Bible stories and amusing them with fun and games. All this dispels the suggestion of intellectual aloofness and a lack of maternal feminine instincts.

Edith was the seventh child of Siegfried and Auguste Stein (four more little ones had not survived). She was born in 1891 on 12 October, the Day of Atonement, one of the major festivals in the Jewish calendar, and it was for this reason, Edith believed, that she was especially dear to her mother. Before she had reached her second birthday, her father died suddenly and unexpectedly. This had a major impact on the life of the Stein family. Auguste had to take on the task of breadwinner as well as mother and immediately stepped into her husband's shoes by running the family business, a timber yard. Inevitably this took her away from home for the majority of every day. Edith and Erna – her sister, eighteen months her senior – were left in the care of the older members of the family. It is likely that a child with as sensitive a nature as Edith suffered more than anyone realized from the daily absence of her mother and the lack of a father. She describes herself as small and anaemic and she constantly suffered from infections and fevers which drained her physical strength. She lived in a hidden world where she brooded over unhappy scenes which she had witnessed or heard about. She found herself unable to share her turmoil with anyone and this surely contributed to the fevers. At the same time, she was a bright, precocious child who enjoyed the company of her bookworm older brother, Paul, who encouraged her to learn long ballads by heart and then to recite them. This was before she could read or write. The frail 'tot' became cocky, and kindergarten, to where she was sent, was considered beneath her dignity. A student boyfriend of an older sister rented their front parlour. In return for assistance with his studies, he would dress the 'tot' before leaving for University. 'Why, Edith!' he exclaimed one day, 'You are like a cow's tail – you grow down instead of up!' Edith did not appreciate her small stature being ridiculed in this way and was more than a little miffed.

While she was a lively precocious child, she was also stubborn and given to angry outbursts when she did not get her own way. As her sixth birthday approached, the only birthday present she longed for was to go to the 'big school' with Erna. Her oldest sister, Else, finally persuaded the school to accept her six months early and she responded to the favour by being an overzealous pupil and was soon near the top of her class. A year further on, she remembers deciding to call a halt to her tantrums, realizing she was letting herself down by behaving in this way. She tells us that: 'early in life I arrived at such a degree of self-mastery that I could preserve my equanimity almost without a struggle'. This was an early indication of her strong will power.

School is for learning and this was Edith's highest objective in life. She was immediately at home in the school environment, and while she was ambitious and pleased to be gaining good marks, receiving prizes and approbation did not appeal to her. This was the only period in her life when she did not make close friends. Her classmates resented her cleverness and it appeared to set her apart.

Edith and Erna grew up like twins, sharing everything, and their devotion and loyalty to each other continued to the end of Edith's life. She remembered their games of hide-and-seek in the timber yard. And the Sunday family excursions when a huge wagon was rented for the day (was it horse-drawn, I wonder?) and the entire family, including various cousins, clambered aboard before setting off for the woods and a glorious picnic. These were happy times but there were others less so which affected them all deeply; more than one family business failure followed by suicide; unsuccessful marriages; the death of a loved aunt from cancer, and of little nephew Harald at two years of age.

Music was important to the Stein children as they grew up, and most of them spent time at the piano which Edith never mastered, for lack of time and incentive, I fancy. Nonetheless, she acquired a love and understanding of classical music which she enjoyed at every opportunity. She was a keen tennis-player and a good dancer. She was full of daydreams of fame and happiness and of one day achieving something great. She and her friend Käthe shared deep discussions on questions ignored in school and engaged in a serious search for 'truth', something which was to evade Edith for many years to come.

Auguste Stein did not impose the practice of her Jewish faith on any of her children but was most faithful to it herself. They were inclined to join her at the synagogue for the major holy days, and when she remained there for long periods of prayer, they would meet her outside the synagogue to accompany her home. Edith describes the preparation for the festivals in great detail and remembers these occasions as a welcome interruption to the daily routine. She was especially attracted to her 'own' Day of Atonement, which demanded a twenty-four-hour fast. From the age of thirteen she observed this fully, even when she no longer shared her mother's faith.

To the dismay of her mother and her tutors, at the age of fifteen she asked to leave school and discontinue her studies. Unbeknown to herself and those around her, she was mentally exhausted. She was, she said, fed up with learning.

As always, her request was acceded to and plans were made for her to travel to Hamburg to be with her sister Else who was expecting her second child and would welcome some help. A six-week return ticket was bought, but in the event Edith stayed for ten months. Her principal task was caring for two-and-a-half-year-old Ilse. Surprisingly, leaving home was no more difficult for Edith than saying farewell to school and friends had been. She describes her existence in Hamburg like that of 'a chrysalis in a cocoon'. When her household duties were complete, she read voraciously from her brother-in-law Max's library. Neither he nor Else had any belief and there was no religion in the house. 'Deliberately and consciously, I gave up praying here,' she tells us. She admits to being apathetic intellectually during these months, but physically she improved rapidly. She thrived in the environment of freedom from study and the pressures of family life in Breslau. The signal for her to return was the serious illness and death of little Harald. Only then did Edith have to consider her future.

On her return to Breslau, Edith took her share of the household duties and the remainder of the time she read to her heart's content. Shakespeare became her daily bread. She happily gave Erna help with her studies but did not consider returning to them herself. Her family tried to interest her in art school or a course in photography, but neither appealed to her.

Eventually she came round to the idea of trying to gain admittance to the grammar school the following year. In order to do this, she required private tuition in mathematics and Latin. Tutors came to the house, each for an hour a day. The rest of the time she became totally absorbed in her homework. Always the true student, she could do this without anyone standing over her. Mathematics she considered an enjoyable sport, a healthy form of exercise. Latin, on the other hand, had a strong appeal and became as it were her 'mother tongue'. Little did she realize what an important role it would have in her life one day. French, English and geography had to be revised. By the following spring, she was well prepared and did not have a problem passing the entrance examination.

In the same year, her reports found her at the top of her class and any joy at this was dispelled by her tutor who warned her not to become complacent. On recounting this to her sister, she burst into tears exclaiming: 'What a conceited goose he must take me to be'. At the same time, to her embarrassment, he used her as a role model for the rest of the class. To have a student who outstripped her classmates, and who was over-confident, appeared to present him with a problem. Nonetheless, by and large these were happy times. To achieve a high standard was always her goal, and work on her essays was a fulfilling challenge. Time was found for visits to the theatre where she enjoyed classical opera as well as the great tragedies. Tobogganing or a hike into the hills with a picnic were a regular relief from study.

The time came for further examinations if she wished to move on to the University, which by now she was determined to do. As usual, the exams did not present a problem, but deciding which subjects she would choose when entering the University was a different matter. The family threw up their hands in dismay at literature and philosophy. How had she come by the idea of philosophy, they wondered? When asked by cousin Richard, 'Why philosophy?', she replied asking, 'Why mathematics for him?' A short comment by herself suggests the subject appealed to her and that she was confident she had the necessary talents to pursue it: 'We are in the world to serve humanity . . . this is best accomplished when doing that for which one has the requisite talents.'

In her twentieth year on 27 April 1911, Edith scanned the bulletin boards in the narrow hallway of Breslau University in order to choose which lectures she would attend. She had arrived at the seat of learning and was full of happy expectation. She spent the next four semesters studying under Stern and Hönigswald. Her primary aim was to gain knowledge, but to pass the state board examinations, a teaching qualification, she considered less important. However, she realized that as a serious student, this was required of her. She was also aware how proud her mother would be if she succeeded. The freedom of choice regarding the lectures had its drawbacks and she had no one to guide her in this. Her mother's best advice was to follow her own judgment, which she did. Her daily schedule became crowded, but she tells us she 'swam in delight as a fish does in clear water and warm sunshine'. She joined the Prussian Society for Women's Right to Vote and made many close and lasting friendships. Rose Guttmann was one of them. It was she who introduced Edith to a Pedagogical Group which had been formed among the students. Edith acquired a high regard for their leader, Hugo Hermsen. She joined the Women's Student Union, undertook private tutoring for others, and entered fully into the Centenary celebrations of the University. It was indeed her Alma Mater.

As I turned the pages of *Life in a Jewish Family* I discovered that Edith did not spare herself criticism when casting her thoughts back to life at home in this period. She invariably arrived home late at night and rarely shared a meal with the family. She became detached from their concerns and even considered herself beyond the reproach of her dear mother. She was living in a heady philosophical world in which all else was submerged and in which she excelled. She says: 'I lived only for my studies and the aspirations they had awakened in me'. It is apparent she had become supercilious and had little time for mortals lesser than herself.

At the Pedagogical Group she met Georg Moskiewiz – Mos to his friends – a highly qualified thirty-three-year-old who was working on his thesis. It was he who introduced Edith to the work of Edmund Husserl. She soon became totally engrossed in Husserl's writings and spent a Christmas vacation in the library reading from the only copy of his work available.

From this, the idea of spending a semester at Göttingen to study under Husserl was kindled, and the flame was lit by an invitation from her cousin Richard Courant and his wife to join them there. Her mind was made up and she determined this was to be her next step. As always, her mother supported her wishes, saying: 'If you need to go there to study, I certainly won't bar your way.' But she was very sad – much sadder than a short absence for a summer's semester warranted. Edith, however, 'was able to sever the seemingly strongest ties with minimal effort and fly away like a bird escaped from a snare'. Nonetheless, deep in her heart she shared her mother's anxiety that it would be an incisive parting. When she came to say goodbye to Hermsen, he remarked: 'I wish you the good fortune of finding in Göttingen people who will satisfy your taste. Here you seem to have become far too critical.' Edith was stunned, unaccustomed as she was to any form of criticism. She had, she said, 'been living in the naïve conviction that [she] was perfect'. Such words from a man she respected caused her acute distress . . . 'Nor did I shrug them off as an undeserved reproach. They were for me a first alert to which I gave much reflection.'

It is apparent that during her studies in Breslau, Edith had emerged from the 'cocoon' in which she had lived in Hamburg. In her thirst for knowledge, it was as if she was travelling on a train with no stations, no stops – nothing was to interrupt her progress. Nonetheless she maintained her high ideals, her sense of indebtedness to the state for 'free access to the wisdom of mankind' and to her childhood understanding that it was more important to be good than clever. She was, after all, her mother's daughter.

It is noticeable that faith and God were given no consideration in this period of Edith's life. They were placed in a hidden recess of her mind from where they would only emerge as her search for the truth bore fruit, step by slow step.

CHAPTER TWO

Göttingen and its Legacy

Edith's memories of Göttingen are encapsulated in one word, 'Dear', and it is abundantly clear that she cherishes her time spent there. As I explored the streets of Göttingen in her company, I was consumed with a sense of having 'been there' and of having shared those first early happy days with her. I travelled beside her up the narrow streets of the *Marktplatz* listening to the toll of the Angelus Bells of St Alban's church. I shared a torte with her in the famous pastry shop of *Kron und Lanz* and discovered the Philosophical Seminar room just below the roof of a modern elegant building. I entered the lecture hall, the very centre of University life, and read the commemorative plaques on the older houses which held a special attraction for Edith.

Inevitably, her exploring led her beyond the town and to the village of Nikolausberg which sits on the top of a mountain and whose Inn offered excellent waffles. To the left of this village, Edith tells us, 'rose a bare hill crowned with three windswept trees which always reminded me of the three crosses on Golgotha'. How was this, I ponder? One of the many joys of Edith's first semester was the companionship of her friend from Breslau, Rose Guttmann. They shared rooms and much of their leisure time. It was their habit to pack a rucksack with a loaf of pumpernickel, a jar of butter, some cold cuts, fruit and chocolate and set off for a day of total freedom. They discovered the parks, the forest, Thuringia, Weimar and Jena. Even the soil, which did not cling to their boots as the clay she was used to had done, leaves a fond memory.

All this provides the backdrop to phenomenology, the object of her visit, and the many new friendships she made. Before she left Breslau, Mos advised her that her first contact on arrival at Göttingen should be Adolf Reinach. This was Professor Husserl's right-hand man and his link with the students. Edith's visit to his home and meeting with him filled her with happiness and gratitude. She had not anticipated such a warm welcome from a complete stranger. She decided not to call on Husserl in the same way, but attended a preliminary discussion, announced by him on the bulletin board; this was when newcomers were expected to present themselves for acceptance. She describes him as 'being as real as he can be'. I am not certain what she means by this but suggest that his great mind and intellect hid the personality of the man whom she never truly 'knew'. Husserl was astonished to learn she had read both volumes of his *Logical Investigations* and immediately accepted her as one of his students. To them, he was 'the Master' and Edith often refers to him in this way.

The Göttingen Philosophical Society was a select group chaired by Mos, Edith's friend from Breslau. It was he who invited Edith and Rose to join the Society. They were unaware how privileged they were to be included, at such an early stage in their studies, and Edith recalls being impudent enough to engage in the discussions immediately. She describes other members of the Society, remembering that Hans Lipps made a deeper impression on her than the rest. Two more from the group became good friends: Erika Gothe and Fritz Kaufmann. Many of the young phenomenologists were influenced by the writings of Max Scheler and he was invited to lecture to their group. Edith attended his lectures, with some reservations, because Scheler was at odds with Husserl's thinking in certain regards and Edith was always essentially loyal to the Master. Nonetheless, Scheler had an influence on her beyond the sphere of philosophy on account of his Catholic faith, to which he had recently returned after a period of lapsing. He was full of Catholic ideas presenting an unknown world to Edith and opening a region of phenomena which she could not bypass blindly. However, she decided she was unable to embark on investigating the questions of faith because she was far too busy with other matters: 'I was content to accept without resistance the stimuli coming from my surroundings, and so, almost without noticing it, became gradually transformed.' Edith's cousin, Richard Courant, and his wife, Nelli, were her good friends. Their door was always open and a welcome assured. She was equally fond of them both and it was a source of great grief to her when their marriage broke down some time later.

Edith's studies knew no bounds and early on she had registered to attend Max Lehmann's seminars in order to follow her other chosen subject, history. She worked hard on a paper on the Draft Constitution of 1849 which so impressed Lehmann that he offered to accept it as a submission for the state boards. This was a total surprise to Edith who had expected to take these from Breslau, but only *after* she had achieved a doctorate, which had become her all-important objective.

At the same time, the thought of leaving Göttingen, not to return, had become intolerable. Lehmann's offer gave her a very good reason for returning. One could not, after all, let a completed board thesis go to waste! Added to which, it was her earnest desire to continue work with Husserl. On receiving a blessing from Professor Stern of Breslau, Edith went to Husserl to discuss a doctoral theme. 'You mean you are ready for that?' he asked in some surprise. After advising her that it would take three years, and telling her not to put her state boards on one side, he agreed to her chosen subject of Empathy.

At vacation time, her welcome home was a loving one with no opposition to her plans to return to Göttingen. She was equally well received by the professors and her old friends at Breslau University, and was able to join in the celebrations being held for the centenary of the War of Independence.

By October, she was back in Göttingen, this time without Rose, and Edith admits to missing her company and feeling lonely. Her study progressed apace, and being free to attend Reinach's lectures on a regular basis was, she says, 'pure joy'. The hours spent at his 'exercises', when it was the students' habit to enjoy a mutual searching with Reinach as their guide, were some of the happiest she spent. On the darker side, her study load became too great as she revised for her oral state exams and was obliged to add Greek to her curriculum. In addition, she pored over Theodor Lipps' philosophical works on Empathy. Her eating habits were irregular, her hours of work too long, and sleep began to elude her. She worked herself into a state of veritable despair. She writes: 'For the first time in my life I was confronted by something I could not conquer by sheer will-power. Subconsciously, my mother's maxims: "What one wants to do, one can do," and "As one strives, so will God help" had become firmly entrenched in me.' Poor Edith, these were the first cracks in her self-sufficiency. Her occasional discussions with Husserl, concerning her work's progress, brought no relief and she found herself fighting a solitary battle. Her friendship with Hans Lipps and the time she spent with him were a relief from the strain, as were the occasional social gatherings. It was some time before Edith had the opportunity to meet Anna Reinach, Adolf's wife. Once she had, her friendship with them both deepened. A growing awareness of their strong Christian convictions and their close marriage left a deep impression. She tells us Adolf's lectures invariably concluded 'Finished thank God' and that Anna's welcome to his students was a warm one. A Christmas supper spent with the Reinachs was a happy memory.

Edith joined her mother in Hamburg, at the home of her sister, Else, for the Christmas vacation. It was not a happy visit, with an obvious crisis in the marriage of her brother-in-law and sister. On her return to Göttingen, at the suggestion of her friend Mos, Edith determined to ask Reinach for his advice on her work. This required a personal meeting, outside the student group, but Reinach immediately placed himself at her disposal. After going through the mass of material she had acquired, he encouraged her to go ahead and draft a text. She immediately set about the task which had frustrated her for so long. When she returned to Reinach with the completed text, he congratulated her and said Husserl was sure to be pleased with it. Edith tells us she 'was like one reborn'.

The following vacation at Breslau was absorbed by family affairs. Erna was in the midst of her medical state boards, and to support her through this ordeal was important. It was decided that Else should come home to Breslau for a visit in the hope of repairing the marriage. Edith offered to travel to

Hamburg to bring her and the children home. It was a delicate task but Edith insisted that her earlier relationship with this family ensured she was best suited to do so. Her own concerns were thrust firmly into the background.

Before returning to Göttingen for her third term, Edith made a new friend in Breslau, Toni Meyer. Toni was preparing to join the Husserl Phenomenology School and Edith was asked to give her lessons in advance. In Göttingen, Toni became a caring friend who offered Edith kindness and support. In her usual way, Edith overworked and cared little for her physical well-being. Toni's thoughtfulness provided a welcome balance to her punishing regime, and it seems she filled the gap which Rose had left. This term also saw the arrival of Pauline Reinach, Adolf's sister, for her first University term. She soon became a firm friend, whom Edith describes as lively and witty but with a deeply contemplative nature.

Student life was rolling peacefully along when the world was shattered by the assassination of Crown Prince Ferdinand and his wife in Sarajevo. It seemed certain that war in Europe would follow, as indeed it did. Richard Courant and Adolf Reinach were two of the first to volunteer for army service. Edith, Nelli and Toni made plans to return to Breslau without delay. Edith, ever the patriot, was anxious to place herself at her country's service. When she said goodbye to Reinach, he suggested they keep in touch, and for the the first time she recognized that he valued her as a friend and not just as one of his students. She had, apparently, not 'presumed' this and it must have provided a source of happiness in spite of the parting.

Upon her return to Breslau Edith undertook a nursing course and thereafter placed herself at the disposal of the Red Cross. After three months in Breslau it became clear there was no immediate place for her in the war effort. Her subsequent nursing service in Austria in 1915 belongs to another segment of her life, another chapter, which follows later.

In October, she decided to return to Göttingen and resume studies for her oral exams. Nelli placed the deserted Courant apartments at her disposal and this was luxury indeed. Domesticity was never very high on Edith's agenda and she soon found help with keeping the rooms clean and the central heating going. Her mother, well aware of her daughter's failings, sent her a regular weekly packet. It contained her home-baked 'Sabbath' bread, a goose liver and other little delicacies.

One of the most endearing features of Edith's autobiography is the ease with which she transports her reader into the room which she is describing. I find myself sinking into the upholstered sofa in Reinach's study or perching on a corner of the long leather one in Husserl's (the latter accommodated many students as their conversation flowed up and down it), or better still, sitting upright behind Richard Courant's large oak desk surrounded by windows through which both sunrise and sunset could be enjoyed.

Few of her fellow students remained in Göttingen, but an exception was two good friends, Erika Gothe and Pauline Reinach. When Edith reflects on these times, she remembers them as some of her happiest in Göttingen, in spite of the overriding anxiety of the war. She writes: 'The friendship with Pauline and Erika had more depth and beauty than my former student friendships. For the first time, I was not the one to lead or to be sought after; but rather I saw in the others something better and higher than myself.' It was a rare time of companionship as she studied philosophy with Erika, Homer with Pauline, and in the evening they joined together to knit socks or prepare Christmas parcels for the boys at the front. Husserl's seminars had few students that winter, 1914, and Edith found herself free from distractions and able to concentrate on her own work. Her thesis was submitted in November and her oral exams booked for mid-January. She determined to remain on her own in Göttingen over Christmas to prepare for them. Her friends brought her a decorated Christmas tree as a parting gift. Neither the tree nor Christmas held any significance for her, but on this occasion, she did not experience loneliness.

Edith confesses to grave misgivings and anxieties before the orals but once confronted by the examiners, her confidence returned and she relished the challenge. She passed with highest honours, and celebrations with friends and Husserl ensued. A telegram home was greeted with congratulations but with her mother's reservation: 'she would be even happier were I to be mindful of the One to whom I owed this success. But for me it had not come to that yet.' While many of Edith's friends were Christians, and she occasionally accompanied them to church, she tells us she had not yet found her way back to God. But for the first time she had come to respect questions of faith and those who had faith. The twenty-three-year-old was slowly growing in maturity, tolerance and an open mind. Edith remained in Göttingen until the end of that term (Spring 1915) brushing up her Greek and working on her doctorate. Before leaving Göttingen, she shipped all her possessions home, thinking she was unlikely to return. Did she sever seemingly strong ties with minimal effort on this occasion, I wonder?

Shortly before Christmas the same year, she received an invitation from Pauline Reinach to join them in Göttingen. Her brother Adolf was due home on furlough and would be celebrating his birthday. One can imagine the joy as Edith left Breslau, with the blessing of her family. This visit was a time rich in reunions and celebrations. She was able to spend valuable hours with Husserl, reviewing her work for her doctorate and gaining his approval of it. The time spent with the Reinachs was golden and she was admitted to the circle of 'mourners of the first rank'. In semi-jest, Reinach alluded to the possibility of his death in the war and Edith joined Anna, Pauline and Erika in the 'first rank'.

Her cousin, Richard Courant, claimed a good deal of her time. He was in the midst of his divorce and needed to share his pain and the reasons for it. Edith had already heard Nelli's account of their disagreements and lent her sympathetic ear to them both, sharing in their unhappiness. From this time on, Edith's visits to Göttingen were occasional. A short stopover is mentioned on the very last page of her manuscript. She had just received her doctorate in 1916 at Freiburg and was returning to Breslau via Göttingen. As I look at the map, I wonder if this was the most direct train journey home or whether it was planned in order to have a few hours with Anna Reinach who met her at the station? Edith's time on her 'Life' ran out before she could tell us.

Adolf Reinach was killed at the front in 1917. This was a devastating blow to those closest to him. Edith compared her own grief to that of his widow and wondered how she could console her when they met. In the event Anna's calm and courageous acceptance was a lesson which Edith never forgot.

Anna's faith in the face of deepest sorrow provided Edith with one of the first important steps towards conversion. Many years later, she confided to a priest friend: 'It was my first encounter with the Cross and the divine power that it bestows on those who carry it. For the first time, I was seeing with my very eyes the Church, born from its Redeemer's sufferings, triumphant over the sting of death. That was the moment my unbelief collapsed.'

Anna asked Edith to assist her in putting Adolf's philosophical work in order. This she considered a privilege and a way of repaying the debt she owed her former tutor and friend. She firmly rejected her family's suggestion that she was spending too much time away from her own work in order to do this. Her letters tell us she spent two periods in Göttingen in 1918, in April and August, working on Reinach's literary legacy. That she returned again in June/July 1919 to continue the work is apparent from further letters. At the same time, she was pursuing her own objective of *Habilitation*, the second qualification leading to a Professorship, at Göttingen University. On 8 November 1919, she wrote to Fritz Kaufmann to say: 'For all of ten days, the rejection, in black and white, has been in my pocket . . . [the application] was not even taken up by the faculty, but was quietly dispatched.' Imagine the disappointment and hurt. A letter written to Fritz two weeks later is appreciative of his concern for her but goes on to say: 'I am no longer the least bit furious or sad . . . After all, I do not consider life on the whole to carry so much weight that it would matter a great deal what position I occupy. And I would like you to make that attitude your own.'

At the end of May 1920, a further letter to Fritz tells him she will be in Göttingen in August to meet Erika Gothe and Hans Lipps. She was there once more in March 1921. Her reason for this visit is unclear but we know she was close to making what she describes as 'the greatest decision of her life' which followed in August of the same year. I searched in vain through Edith's *Self-Portrait in Letters* for correspondence between herself and Anna and Pauline Reinach. They were such close friends with whom she surely kept in touch. They both became Catholics and Pauline a Benedictine nun.

It may appear remiss that the Master, Husserl, receives no more than the occasional mention in this chapter. He was, of course, a very important cog in Edith's life, and her relationship with him will be explored in a separate chapter. Important as he was, the Reinach family were the ones whose friendship provided significant footholds for Edith's footsteps as she trod firmly forward.

Göttingen offered the opportunity for her to satisfy her hunger for knowledge, for her to enjoy friendships of value, to experience a personal freedom in her decisions and to let go of her disappointments. She admits to being transformed, to spending some of the happiest times of her life, to discovering her inability to reach her own high standards at all times. Her pure mind enabled her to perceive there was something, someone beyond and greater than all the learning for which she strove. But that same mind had not yet fully grasped what it was, or indeed allowed itself the space to do so.

The days spent at Göttingen were surely the defining ones in Edith's life.

CHAPTER THREE

Friendships

Edith's capacity for friendship was as great as her capacity for learning. It had no boundaries, and I doubt anyone who sought it was rejected. It is an aspect of Edith's life which drew me to her and through which I came to know her better. Is there a finer way of discerning a person's character than by the quality of their friendship? Edith had a profound respect for, and devotion to, Adolf and Anna Reinach and, as has been seen, her relationship with them was important to her. She made many more enduring friendships among both men and women during her student days at Göttingen. I have chosen to identify those who I believe illustrate best the wide diversity of her friends and her ability to respond loyally to their various needs. In her usual way, Edith's text brings her friends to life. They are real luminous people whose personalities and idiosyncrasies it is easy to share with her.

The Guttmanns were a Breslau family whose daughter Rose was one of three children. She was a student of mathematics, and when she and Edith first met, she already had a good friend, Lilli Platau. As time passed, Lilli became friends with Edith's sister, Erna – they were both medical students – and Edith and Rose came together through their shared interest in philosophy. Ultimately, the four of them 'fused to form an indivisible four-leaf clover'. Edith describes Rose as 'gifted with excellent taste in dress. Her most beautiful adornment however was her hair: two long, glossy black braids worn with simplicity wound around her head.' Rose was a good listener and an easy companion. Edith suggests her intellect was not so great as it was made out to be, but this did not inhibit the growth of their friendship. Edith was the youngest member of the clover leaf and was known as 'chick', and yet it was invariably she who planned the excursions and celebrations. The four girls were not exclusive in their clover leaf and were often joined by friends and other members of their family.

Rose suffered from heart strain and Edith was concerned for her health when she overworked. It was necessary for her to earn her own student fees by tutoring in her spare time. How good it would be, Edith thought, if Rose could join her as she made plans for her first term in Göttingen. She asked her mother if she was rich enough to support student fees for Rose as well as for herself. While her mother was able and pleased to do so, it did not prove necessary. What a happy arrangement it was for the two girls to spend their first term away from home together. They rented rooms using one as a shared bedroom and the other as an excellent living room cum study. When possible, they shared classes even though their main subjects were not the same. They spent all their free time together, exploring the new town and countryside, and when Edith returned to Göttingen for her second term without Rose, she experienced great loneliness.

Four years later in 1917, the clover leaf was reunited when Erna, Rose and Lilli travelled to Freiburg during their vacation in order to spend time with Edith. Erna tells us – in her contribution to the 'Editors' Foreword' to Edith's *Life* – that they discussed the issue of marriage and whether one should be prepared to give up a career for marriage. Edith herself tells us: 'The other three married but, nevertheless, continued in their careers. I alone did not marry, but I alone have assumed an obligation for which, joyfully, I would willingly sacrifice any other career.'

I was sad to find no reference to Rose in Edith's letters. I do not believe the clover leaf withered and died but rather that it lived on as the lives of the four girls moved in different directions.

Edith's friendship with Eduard Metis was, as far as I can tell, her first with a young man of her own age. Eduard was an orthodox and observant Jew and the only child of an over-protective affectionate mother. He was a tall, slim young man who was both sensitive and upright. He did not enjoy good health and often suffered from migraine. Edith met Eduard at Breslau University when he was chairman of the academic branch of the Humboldt Society. At their first encounters he did not impress Edith greatly, and it was only when he became her study partner that she grew to appreciate his many virtues.

After an end-of-term *Sommerfest* Edith found herself making the journey home with Eduard. They walked most of the way catching a tram for the final stretch. When they parted company, Eduard remarked that, for him, her company on the way back had been the happiest part of the day. Shortly afterwards, Edith received a note asking her to call on him to discuss some Humboldt business. The business amounted to very little and Edith realized it had been an excuse to ask her to join him for a walk. She noticed that it required considerable courage for him to extend the invitation, which she gladly accepted. This was followed by further overtures and Edith felt it was only fair to make her position clear. Their relationship could not be extended beyond friendship and he should relinquish any further expectations. This situation was graciously accepted by Eduard, and from then on he respected her wishes most faithfully. They met on an almost daily basis and began the study of Gothic German together. A weekly walk was enjoyed by them both and Edith writes of Eduard as 'a fine young man'.

Eduard was a journalist who undertook regular book reviews. Edith read these with pleasure until one day she found his frivolous comments on some erotic material in a volume of novellas unacceptable. Edith's usual high principles could not let this pass, and she read him a sermon saying their friendship would have to cease. Eduard was deeply embarrassed and confessed the frivolous attitude had been used in order to get the task over and done with in the quickest possible way. Edith did not doubt his sincerity and the matter was put behind them. Eduard's strict observance of his religion was another source of embarrassment. To carry Edith's briefcase in the street on the Sabbath was not permissible and he could not move out of the doorway with it in his hands. This was, Edith says, 'an example of the talmudic sophistry which I found so repugnant'. She did not however allow her friend to see her distaste for such things. When Edith moved to Göttingen, she and Eduard maintained a weekly correspondence, and in her vacations they came together again in the study of German literature. Eduard gained his doctorate at his second attempt and Edith attended his graduation ceremony where she met his parents for the first time. When later she received her *summa cum laude*, Eduard wrote: 'What was inevitable has come to pass'. Eduard was considered unfit for military service, and when he had passed his state boards, he took up a teaching post. It was a great shock to Edith when she learned Eduard had died of pneumonia while she was away from home in Freiburg. Their friendship had been a pure and wholesome one where a unique openness and honesty between them had prevailed.

Mos – Dr Georg Moskiewicz – was not, I believe, a close friend of Edith's but he was certainly an influential one. It was he who introduced her to Husserl's *Logical Investigations* and who later gave her a personal introduction to Reinach.

Mos was the son of a wealthy Jewish businessman, and when Edith first met him he was thirty-three years old and already had an M.D. and a Ph.D. to his name. He had studied medicine to please his father but had transferred his interests to philosophy and psychology. Edith describes him as having reddish hair, light blue eyes with a pale complexion and nervous tendencies. He was unhappy in his position as chairman of the philosophical society in Breslau. The students made fun of his lack of confidence and he had to rely on the support of his good friend, Hans Lipps.

Before his arrival in Breslau, Mos had studied in Göttingen for one year and he longed to return. When he heard that Edith and Rose had plans to go there, he determined to join them and the girls welcomed this. Edith makes special mention of the birthday celebrations which they arranged for him and the fact that he was strongly attracted to Rose.

When Edith returned to Göttingen in 1914 without a companion, she was grateful for his company and regularly forgave him for his unreliability. So often, arrangements made between them for meetings or walks were broken at the last moment occasionally, only to be remade later. Edith realized it was difficult for Mos to commit himself to anything and excused his behaviour by saying that phenomenology was his unrequited love. Reinach offered Mos some private lessons and Edith was alarmed when he confided to her how unendurable he found these sessions with Mos and how he would like to bring them to an end. Edith persuaded Reinach that this would be a terrible shock to Mos and that it would be likely to increase his lack of confidence in himself. Reinach took heed of Edith's concern for her friend and the matter later resolved itself when Mos moved to Frankfurt.

When Edith returned from her nursing service, she found Mos working as Chief Resident in a Breslau asylum where his medical duties allowed him little time to pursue his interest in philosophy. He was frustrated both in this and in his devotion to Rose Guttmann which he felt unable to resolve. While Mos had such great difficulty in deciding things for himself, he certainly influenced Edith in the progress of her philosophical career. It was Mos to whom Edith confided her anguish over her lack of progress on her thesis. It was his wise advice that she should go to Reinach for help which finally resolved her crisis. Edith was remarkably tolerant of Mos's shortcomings and was always a good and wise friend to those who suffered from any form of human weakness.

Toni Meyer is another example of Edith's compassion and her ability to empathize with those who were not necessarily her chosen compatible companions. Toni was introduced to Edith by their mutual friends, Rose and Mos. She was a Breslau girl who lived with her mother in a house which gave the appearance of wealth. When Edith shared a meal with them, she admired the fine porcelain and linens which were used. A portrait of Toni as a child revealed a delicate vivacious little girl, but at the age of thirty-six, her heavy features indicated great suffering and she had difficulty in walking. Edith was 'engaged' to give Toni lessons in advance of her first term at Göttingen and she felt that Mrs Meyer paid her more than she was worth. On account of her poor health, Toni's studies demanded great courage and Edith admired her for this.

Toni's time in Göttingen was one of the happier periods of her life. Edith introduced her to the Philosophical Society and she was able to attend the lectures without her usual bouts of depression. One day, Toni confided to Edith that she suffered from mental illness. She was fearful it would destroy or weaken their friendship. She did not know Edith very well to entertain such fears. They often shared an evening meal or a weekend walk and it seems that Edith's firm friendship gave Toni the sense of security which she so badly needed. In return, it was Toni's pleasure to arrange flowers in Edith's room to welcome her home after a long day's study. At the outbreak of war, Toni returned to Breslau with Edith and later transferred her studies to Munich. This was not a success and her health broke down yet again.

In between her further studies at Göttingen and her time away nursing, Edith was at home in Breslau and Toni constantly turned to her for company when she would speak to no one else. Both she and her mother were happy in the family home of the Steins where Auguste made them as welcome as did Edith herself. At one time Edith encouraged Toni to form a small study group in phenomenology in her own home, but finally her health broke down irreparably and she was diagnosed as a manic depressive. After her mother's death she was placed in the care of Franciscan nuns.

I would hardly have chosen Fritz Kaufmann for inclusion in this chapter were it not for Edith's copious correspondence with him. In her *Life*, he is rarely referred to, and half a page sums up her first impressions of him. Indeed, I wonder if this friendship grew out of their correspondence in which they shared their philosophical interests. Edith met Fritz Kaufmann at Göttingen's Philosophical Society where he stood out from the remainder of the students in both his dress and general demeanour. He was the third son of a wealthy Leipzig family and was the only member of their circle in Göttingen whose private means enabled him to pursue his career with no immediate care for his future employment. His dress was elegant and his High German accent gave the impression of affectation. As Edith came to know him, she realized his sophisticated exterior resulted in poor relationships with nearly everybody he met. She took it upon herself to tease him and, in her own words, 'to thaw him out'. She was surprised to learn that even the kind, mild-mannered Reinach had taken offence at his high-handed approach and had refused to admit him to his classes. Fritz arrived in Göttingen with a philosophical background in which he took pride, and no doubt this was displayed and caused offence.

Soon after Edith and Rose arrived in Göttingen they decided to make their first visit to the Bismarck Tower. They were picking violets on the way when they were joined by Fritz. He greeted them and remarked in a friendly way: 'There are plenty of violets here.' Many months later, when Fritz was away on active service and the Christmas parcels for the boys were being wrapped, his were tied with violet-coloured ribbon. I am sure this was intended to revive memories of happier days.

Fritz's war service took him to the Eastern Front and the Rumanian conflict. It is remarkable that three of Edith's letters written then have survived. She wrote to keep him in touch with her life in Freiburg and in 1918, when he was awaiting demobilisation in the barracks in Rumania, she told him of her break with the Master.

Letters written after his demob read rather like that of an elder sister, though in reality their birth dates were within a few months of each other. She encouraged him to wait patiently until the mood for work returned, and it appears they were each concerned for the other's welfare.

Fritz eventually returned to Freiburg where he was awarded his doctorate. His friendship with Edith subsequently had to survive two crises. The first seems to have been a genuine misunderstanding and was resolved after letters of explanation. The second was much more serious and followed Edith's conversion. As a fellow Jew, Fritz must have felt very strongly against this move of Edith's and they were estranged for nearly five years. The loss of his friendship at such a sensitive time was surely a source of sadness for her. In spite of this, it was she who broke the silence when she heard of his mother's illness. She wrote: 'yesterday, while putting old letters in order, I came across several of yours. These – I cannot say "reminded me of you" since forgetting has never been my thing where human relations are concerned – but [the letters] moved you out from the fog-shrouded distance into palpable nearness again, and I wanted to tell you that.' Their correspondence was renewed at the right time because Fritz suffered the loss of his mother shortly afterwards.

Edith resumed the sisterly approach and invited him to visit her at Speyer. We do not know whether he did so, but to show they were fully reconciled, he visited her twice in Cologne Carmel.

Fritz married and he and his family eventually settled in the USA. When his first wife died, Fritz remarried, and it was his second wife who bequeathed all Edith's letters to the Cologne Carmel archive. Fritz died in Zürich in 1958.

Edith's first impressions of Erika Gothe were not auspicious. Erika and her friend, Grete Ortmann, came from the region of Mecklenburg and were already well-established members of the Philosophical Society when Edith and Rose arrived in Göttingen. They were qualified teachers undertaking further studies and were of an older age group. It is obvious that from the outset there was a personality clash between Grete Ortmann and Edith. Reinach was well aware of this and took Grete to task for her unfriendly attitude to Fräulein Stein 'who is . . . so nice'. Grete's retort to Reinach was: 'She simply joins in every discussion. And that even though they're such difficult matters!' A little jealousy, maybe? Erika's respectful silence was more encouraging, but as she and Grete were inseparable, they failed to draw Edith and Rose into their tightly-knit group.

When Edith returned to Göttingen for her third term during the war, she discovered Erika was the only member of Husserl's closer circle to be there. There was no mention of Grete, nor indeed is there again, apart from a brief reference to a visit she made to Husserl in Freiburg some time later. In her absence, Edith and Erika easily drifted together and were often joined by Pauline Reinach. They invariably shared a midday meal at Erika's lodgings and met in Pauline's study in the evenings. Erika had a younger brother, Hans, who was at the Front and she was very concerned for his safety. His Christmas parcels were tied with peasant binding, sporting colourful flowers on a black background, while Reinach's were tied in gold. Erika was one of the four Reinach 'mourners' which is likely to be another reason why she and Edith became good friends.

Like others before her, Erika realized how poorly Edith cared for herself and often prepared a meal for her when she was working late. She was certainly a caring friend and made the journey to Freiburg to be with Edith as she made her final preparations for her doctoral exams. She did not like to think of Edith being on her own at such a stressful time. The Reinachs tried to dissuade her from doing this, thinking her presence would be a distraction. In reality, it was good for Edith to have a friend who encouraged her to take some leisure time. Together they explored Feldberg and Lake Constance and occasionally, heavily laden with books, they climbed the mountain slopes and studied in the open air. Erika was with Edith when she was awarded her doctorate and it was she who encouraged her to offer her services as assistant to Husserl. She shared Edith's joy at the happy outcome of these events and Edith writes: 'Erika looked at me. We needed no exchange of words to reach an understanding. Her deep-set, dark eyes were alight with intense joy.' It was the second occasion on which Edith made special mention of Erika's eyes which apparently expressed so well her pleasure at her friend's happiness.

Between 1917 and 1920, Edith made several visits to Göttingen when she invariably stayed with Erika. Because there are no published letters to Erika, we do not know what became of their friendship after Edith's conversion. In a letter written to Hedwig Conrad-Martius in December 1934 from Cologne Carmel, she wrote: 'Remember me also to Erika and her mother when you have a chance. Are they happy about my being in Carmel?' She sounds a trifle wistful and sad to have lost touch with her old friend.

Edith does not provide a personal portrait of Roman Ingarden and for this reason I do not feel I know him very well. Their friendship appears to have developed after she received her doctorate which is where her *Life* ends. Her copious correspondence with Roman indicates that their relationship was another which was developed and sustained through letter-writing.

Roman was a Polish Catholic who was born in Cracow. He was a member of the Polish Legion until a heart defect forced his retirement. He arrived in Göttingen during the war and was the only member of the old Göttingen circle to follow Husserl to Freiburg. For this reason he was there when Edith was awarded her doctorate, and it was he, together with Erika, who celebrated with her in the evening after the examination. I do not doubt their friendship grew in the following months while Roman continued his studies and Edith worked for Husserl.

Only seventeen of the one hundred and sixty extant letters written to Roman by Edith appear in her *Self-Portrait*. The remainder have yet to be translated. In one letter, Edith is very appreciative of Roman's critical appraisal of her work and in another, she writes of her efforts to encourage the Master to read his thesis. Roman was strong in his defence of Edith when she left the Master's employment and once said of her: 'She would never have written or said anything she would not have replicated in her actions.' It is likely their philosophical minds came together in this correspondence. As a Catholic, Roman would have had a greater understanding of Edith's spiritual journey and conversion than most of her friends. He returned to Poland where he introduced phenomenology to the young philosophers of his homeland. Among his students was Karol Wojtyla, now Pope John Paul II. It was at his request, in 1968, that Roman Ingarden delivered a lecture on Edith Stein's philosophy. We are entitled to assume that the Pope's well-known high regard for Edith was originally inspired by this personal friend of hers. Roman married and had four sons, and we learn from a letter, written to Hedwig from Echt in 1940, that Edith was anxious for news of him and his family.

The last in my personal assembly of Edith's friends is Hans Lipps. He was an engaging character for whom Edith had a large soft spot. Whether or not there was any question of her marrying him I am not (unlike some others) prepared to speculate. That he was a much valued friend I am certain.

Hans entered Edith's life in her early days at Göttingen, and she wrote: 'Hans Lipps made a deeper impression on me than did anyone else.' He was twenty-three and she describes him as tall, slim and handsome. He had a serious gaze and large round eyes as inquisitive as a child's. He was a Saxon but insisted he was a Prussian. His life was very full with the study of both medicine and natural science. His creative bent and true insights were attractive to Edith. They were soon friends and enjoyed each other's company.

It became an occasional habit for Edith to join Hans and his companions for lunch or to meet on a one-to-one basis to discuss Edith's work. When she learnt he was leaving Göttingen for Strasbourg, she would, she wrote, 'feel even more forlorn if every prospect of catching a glimpse of his tall figure or of his navy-blue jacket were gone'.

When the war came, and Hans was on military service, it suited him very well. He found the routine of civilian life a 'straitjacket' and once remarked: 'What on earth will I do when peace "breaks out" some day?' Edith was amazed at his ability to carry out his medical studies and at the same time to develop as a philosopher. He could apparently continue his pleasure in the latter as easily in a bunker as in a Göttingen café full of music! Does all this indicate a freedom of spirit and a certain restlessness?

His letters written from the Front were mostly illegible and, according to Husserl, had no content. Edith, on the other hand, wrote that his few words meant a great deal to her and gave her a true picture of his condition. She was able to please him with her choice of gifts for his field packets and appreciated the news of his pet owlet Rebecca.

The last item in Edith's *Life* – before the addendum from Echt – relates 'a very joyous experience' when she met Hans in Dresden. He was on furlough visiting his mother: '[h]e had got heavier during the war and looked splendid in his field-grey uniform with the brown leather leggings.' As they exchanged news, Edith spoke of her work in school and the Latin lessons she was giving. Hans exclaimed: 'Oh, Fräulein Stein, you have no idea how inferior I find myself compared to you.' Edith shook her head: 'How can that possibly be so when you consider this kind of pursuit to be a totally inferior one?' His depths of insight had often given her the sense that all her work was mere 'dabbling'. Their respect for each other was a mutual one.

In February 1918, Edith wrote to Roman Ingarden: '[Lipps] is once more at the Western Front (at his own request).' In May the same year he was slightly wounded and later took part in the Battle of the Marne. From a letter written by Edith in June 1919, we learn that she and Lipps were both in Freiburg. It is about this time that the misunderstanding between herself and Fritz Kaufmann took place and to a degree it concerned Lipps. In her attempts to explain a difficult situation, Edith appears to have misled and maybe hurt Fritz Kaufmann. As usual her honesty prevails and she admits to probably liking Lipps more than Kaufmann. By 1920 all is forgiven and Edith suggests Fritz meets Erika, Hans and herself in Göttingen in August.

The ensuing gap in her letters creates a void in her relationship with Hans but a postcard to Fritz written in November

1925 tells him she had met Hans at Bergzabern – Hatti's – that autumn. We know that Hans married and had two small daughters. His wife died and he remarried. He was finally killed in action in Russia in September 1941.

In a letter written from Echt to the sisters of Beek in November 1941, Edith writes: 'I would also like to beg all the dear Sisters, sincerely, for a memento of a dear friend of mine from our student days [Hans Lipps] who was shot in the head at the Eastern Front. I received the obituary notice yesterday after it had made many detours. He leaves two daughters for whom he was father and mother, since his wife died very early on.' This gives the impression that Edith was unaware that Hans had married for a second time.

Edith did not meet Hedwig Conrad-Martius until 1920. 'Dear Hatti' became her closest friend – but she belongs to another important epoch in Edith's life.

It was inevitable that after her conversion when her life took a new direction, Edith made an entirely new circle of friends, many from the religious life. Her loyalty to her family and her old friends remained as firm as ever.

CHAPTER FOUR

Nurse Edith

Auguste was beaming happily. 'You have never been so obedient!' she exclaimed, little knowing her summons to her youngest daughter to return home immediately had not arrived before Edith left Göttingen. It was, as always, Edith's own decision to return to Breslau. Immediately war appeared imminent, she told herself: 'I have no private life any more . . . All my energy must be devoted to this great happening.'

A nursing course for women students was being organized in Breslau which both Edith and her friend Toni joined on their return. At the same time, Edith placed herself unconditionally at the disposal of the Red Cross. At the conclusion of a four-week course she passed her 'aides' examination. Edith, ever the romantic, had dreams of serving in a field hospital at the front thereafter. She was to be disappointed for there was an oversupply of helpers and she was not called upon. Instead, she remained at the All Saints Hospital in a voluntary capacity gaining further practical experience and spending her evenings poring over Erna's medical textbook. To nurse was not to be a wartime hobby but a task carried out to the best of her ability.

The visible signs of war affected Edith deeply. She recalls the sight of a long string of horses which had been requisitioned for military use. They put her in mind of a large suction pump that was sapping the strength of the land. As did the port of Hamburg, some months later, when it was defunct and in her words it had become 'a forest of cold chimneys and sail-less masts'. Her brothers were not at the front, but cousins and student friends were. Loss of young lives became a reality.

Edith's volunteer work at the hospital was brought to a close by a severe attack of bronchitis. As the autumn term at Göttingen approached and the Red Cross failed to call her up, she decided to return to her studies and prepare for her state boards. It was not until the Spring of 1915 – when her exams were safely behind her – that she received a call from the Red Cross. There were no vacancies for nurses in Germany but there was an urgent need in Austria at an isolation hospital for contagious diseases. Edith did not hesitate to respond to this request in spite of it being against her mother's wishes. For the first time they opposed each other, and she tells us: 'granite was striking granite'. When Auguste provided the nurse's uniform Edith knew she had won the battle.

The hospital was housed in what had been an academy for the cavalry. It was a vast complex of inhospitable adapted buildings. The Matron had one hundred and fifty trained nurses and aides to supervise. Edith's first assignment was to the typhoid ward where baths and disinfectant were a high priority. She soon discovered how inadequate her short training had been and remembered fixing a hot-water bottle for a patient whose teeth were chattering, only to find he was lying in cold icepacks. She and the patient shared a good laugh. After only two weeks, she was placed on night-duty with a ward of sixty typhoid patients under her care. It was here she witnessed death for the first time. After following the normal procedure of calling the doctor and having the body removed, she found herself collecting the patient's few possessions. A small piece of paper slipped from his notebook. It was a prayer for the preservation of his life given him by his wife. Only then, she tells us, 'did I fully realize what this death meant, humanly speaking. But I dared not let myself brood over that. I pulled myself together.'

Edith was appreciated for keeping the ward logbook in good order and for acting as interpreter between the doctor and his patients. The latter came from every nation of the Austro-Hungarian Empire and occasionally from Russia and Turkey.

It is likely Edith was the only one able to familiarise herself with the small nine-language manual supplied. Many of her nursing duties were far from pleasant. Showing her usual sense of purpose and dedication, Edith makes no mention of finding it distasteful. A move to the surgical ward found her involved with operations and dressings of painful wounds. She never spared herself in her efforts to provide extra small comforts for her patients. It appears that her main difficulties were avoiding drink-parties and the unwelcome attentions of a doctor. She felt pretty much alone and made no significant new friendships. She had travelled light with only two books to keep her company, Husserl's *Ideas* and Homer. There was little time for reading, but she was a faithful letter-writer to home and friends.

After three months on the typhoid ward, Edith was entitled to a fifteen-day furlough. She did not take it, feeling she had not earned it. The wards were full and busy and as usual she was totally involved with the job in hand. She had a single day off when her brother Arno visited and again when Erna stayed at the hospital for a week. They enjoyed a good hike in the country but this was little enough time together. She remembered the month of August as very hard. She was often on her feet all day and barely able to stand at the end of it. Overworked as she was, her old habit of being unable to sleep at night plagued her. She lay awake, longing to be back on the ward with her patients. A particularly demanding one finally sapped her remaining strength and she found herself at breaking-point. After considerable problems with her conscience, she asked Matron for leave at the beginning of September. This was granted and when she left she did not consider it to be farewell, fully expecting a recall. This never came and the hospital was closed shortly afterwards. Edith did not hear from the Red Cross again.

Five months is a comparatively short period of time but it is likely it seemed more like five years to Edith. In her *Life*, she portrays her fellow-workers and her suffering patients vividly, and it seems her determination to do her bit saw her through many a difficult situation. She did not complain or think of giving up. Her compassion rose to the surface but it is apparent she had to keep her emotions firmly in check in order to fulfil her duties. The lack of privacy and the absence of her philosophical friends must have been a hardship.

On her return to Göttingen, a friend remarked: 'One can tell just by looking at her that Fräulein Stein has experienced the serious side of life.'

CHAPTER FIVE

The Master

Edmund Husserl was in his fifty-fifth year when Edith first met him in 1913. She describes him as being 'neither striking nor overwhelming' and having the appearance of an elegant professor. He was dignified, of average height and had a handsome head. An Austrian by birth, in Edith's estimation he carried the hallmarks of 'old Vienna'. This was where he had studied. Both the professor and his wife, Frau Malvine, were Jews who had become Evangelical Lutherans. They had three children. Their home in Göttingen on Hohen Weg was built to Frau Malvine's specifications. The Master's study was upstairs with a small balcony where he went to meditate. Frau Malvine was protective of her husband and did not receive all his students as kindly as she did Edith. She had no bond with philosophy and yet she attended all his lectures.

I can picture so well the eager twenty-one-year-old Edith presenting herself to the venerable professor for the first time . . . 'You have read both volumes of *Logical Investigations*? Why, that's a heroic achievement!' he exclaimed. He most surely realized he had an exceptional student standing before him.

It was not long before Edith was finding her way up to Hohen Weg for the professor's 'At Homes'. These were occasions when students were able to present their concerns before joining in lengthy discussions on idealism. There is little doubt in my mind that the professor was no easy man to study under. He was intent on addressing sober, abstract matters and his difficult terminology was described as 'too time-consuming' by one of his students. The same student went on to say: 'Reinach is clearer, but, correspondingly, less deep.' Edith tells us that Husserl took great pains to educate his students to 'rigorous objectivity and thoroughness', to a 'radical intellectual honesty'. How demanding that sounds to the uninitiated like myself.

It appears that Husserl was totally absorbed in his own work, so that it rendered him unable to appreciate the difficulties and limitations of his students. He offered them no short cuts. His insistence that Edith use an analytical dialogue with the work of Theodor Lipps for her doctoral thesis presented a heavy burden which she had to carry on her own until Reinach came to her aid. As she struggled, she was told that Lipps alone was insufficient and she should study all literature available on empathy. This brought on her severe mental strain mentioned in Chapter II when Husserl offered her no help. He was not a good listener and rarely gave his full attention to Edith's questions. She was not the only student to suffer in this way. One of them used the tactic of gaining the professor's attention by joining him on a walk when he would become out of breath and be obliged to listen instead of talking!

Perhaps it was the Master's seeming indifference which deterred Edith from a hasty visit to Hohen Weg with the results of her state board exams. When he heard of them from another source, Edith was in deep trouble. He suggested she might now like to take her doctorate in literature or history since she had done so well. He could not have hurt her more deeply and she let him see this. In order to mollify her, he said, 'Fräulein Stein, you need to get some relaxation. You look completely exhausted.' The situation was not repaired until an invitation was received for Edith and her friends to join the professor and his wife for coffee as a belated celebration on Sunday afternoon. In spite of the obvious irritations and difficulties, Edith remained enthralled by Husserl's lectures and steadfast in her devotion to him. During her absence from Göttingen, whilst she was nursing, the professor's heart appeared to warm a little and their relationship became more cordial. A letter received from him was considered a 'feast' and one lost in the post made Edith miserable.

He was apparently equally well pleased to receive letters from her.

When Edith was in Göttingen for Reinach's birthday, the professor was generous in the time he gave to reviewing the work on her thesis. The Reinachs could not believe he was giving her so much attention. This was most unusual.

Husserl's transfer to Freiburg in 1916 threw all Edith's carefully laid plans into disarray. She would have to follow him in order to take her doctorate. And have to face a fresh set of examiners rather than those under whom she had taken her state boards. Her suggestion to the professor that she might hasten work on her thesis in order to be examined before he left Göttingen was rejected out of hand.

She completed her thesis at home in Breslau. It was typed and ready for despatch to Freiburg during the Easter vacation. It was bound in three volumes in a soft blue cover and was carefully boxed. It had cost her so much toil and pain but now it was complete and on the way to the Master for his judgment. Edith asked him to examine it before she arrived in Freiburg in July but she was warned that he would have little time during his first term. Three months later, when Edith was on her way to Freiburg, she met Hans Lipps in Dresden. She enquired if the Master had read any of her thesis. '[Not] a word' said Hans. Apparently, he occasionally lifted the precious box off the shelf, removed the manuscript, turned it over in his hands, carefully returned it to the box and then to the shelf.

On Edith's arrival in Freiburg, the professor jokingly greeted her with the comment: 'Execution is at hand!' . . . and yet he had not read a single line of her precious work. Frau Malvine was appalled when she heard him tell Edith he had not had time and neither would he. His days were fully employed. Had the new-found warmth disappeared? He suggested Edith remain in Freiburg and attend his lectures and take her doctorate next time. Poor Edith . . . she was totally robbed of her composure but could see no alternative to his proposal.

She had already found herself a room in a comfortable farmhouse in the village of Günterstal in the southern centre of the city, opposite which was a country inn, Zum Kybfelsen, where inexpensive meals were readily available – so handy for the undomesticated Edith. The Husserls were renting a roomy apartment at the foot of the Loretto mountain. All who arrived in their vestibule could see her 'dear Master' at work through a large glass door. This did not afford him the privacy he had been used to at Hohen Weg and he was, Edith said, 'seated as it were in a glass house'. How sensitive to the Master's needs she had become. His suggestion that Edith would be happy to get to know Freiburg and to see how he was settling in, as an alternative to getting her doctorate, showed rather less sensitivity to her needs.

I cannot imagine Edith being long in any city she did not know without exploring it and the surrounding attractions. Her, as yet, unresolved future allowed ample opportunity for getting to know Freiburg.

How lucky for Edith that Frau Malvine was her good friend. She gave her husband no peace until he agreed to find time to read Edith's thesis. Once he finally relented, he gave her leave to go to the dean and make an appointment for her exams, in advance of his own study of the work. This revealed his confidence in her and he was not disappointed. 'I have now got pretty far into your thesis. You really are a very gifted little girl.' Furthermore, he was considering including it in *The Yearbook*, along with his own *Ideas*. 'I have an impression that in your work you forestall some material that is in my second part of *Ideas*.' Could he give her higher praise than this?

Earlier in a private conversation with Edith's friend Erika Gothe, the professor indicated he felt the time had come for him to look for an assistant. The death of his youngest son in the war had left its mark and his eyesight was failing. Could she, Edith, possibly be considered a suitable applicant, she wondered? She did not presume to think so. However, this unsolicited appreciation of her work from the Master gave her the courage to offer her services. The Master's immediate response was: 'You want to help me? Yes! With you, I would enjoy working!' Edith writes: 'I do not know which one of us was more elated. We were like a young couple at the moment of their betrothal.' The fact that he could only offer her one hundred marks a month, insufficient to live on, was not considered important.

Edith was examined for her doctorate on 3 August. It was

a very hot day but she remained cool and confident throughout. She was awarded a *summa cum laude*, the highest grade, a greater honour than she dared to expect. She left Freiburg to complete a teaching engagement in Breslau before returning later in the year as the professor's lady assistant. The prospect pleased her greatly.

Edith's Freiburg memories are the final chapter in her *Life* and were written nearly twenty-five years after the events, by which time she was in Echt Carmel, and yet she records those days as if they were yesterday. I found it easy to forget how much water had flowed under the bridge of her life. They must have been memories full to the brim, of hope and expectation of what she might achieve as the Master's assistant.

To follow the next phase in Edith's life, I have to draw mostly on her letters. She was a great letter-writer and where there are gaps, we can be sure they are only there because the letters have not been retained by the receiver. The second half of her life would have been that much greyer without this very personal archive.

Edith soon discovered the tribulations of being assistant to the Master. She had to learn the Gabelsberger shorthand, gather the papers into some order and follow the learned man's scattered thoughts. As she brought these together, it was necessary to confer with the Master but she was faced with his sudden and variable fancies and his total lack of collaboration. At the same time as failing to listen to her pleas for him to study her work, he was telling her he could not do without her and should she marry, her husband too would have to become his assistant. It is hard to believe anyone could be so lacking in consideration. As she left for a holiday in March 1917, he encouraged her to have a good break at home but could not resist putting his 'Sixth Study' into her hands as she left.

The following term, Edith began her own class in the afternoons for the young students. It was her 'kindergarten' and she filled the role Reinach had done for her and others in Göttingen. She describes the classes as fun but providing her with little stimulus.

The professor promised her he would consider her work on his *Ideas* immediately after Pentecost. By July it remained untouched in her desk. Husserl's promise was not fulfilled. A new manuscript on 'Time Consciousness' revitalised her and she kept working regardless of the professor. The following February (1918), he quite unexpectedly gave Edith a whole set of directions on how to handle his manuscripts. This after she had been working for him for eighteen months with little or no interest being taken in what she had achieved. Finally, Edith decided she could no longer continue as his assistant. Formal letters of notice and acceptance were passed between them. A letter written to a friend says: 'The Master has graciously accepted my resignation . . . though not without a somewhat reproachful undertone. So now I am free, and I believe it is good that I am, even if, for the moment, I am not exactly happy . . .' This surely was an understatement and her sadness at the failure of their working relationship must have been very great.

Edith's subsequent letters reveal no bitterness but only the hope that the professor will not think too badly of her and that she might continue to help him if needed. She was involved with preparing a *Festschrift* for his sixtieth birthday and was willing to travel to Freiburg at any time if called upon. They remained good friends, and it was science's loss that these twin minds did not achieve great results in partnership. The Master was very generous in the recommendation he gave Edith as she endeavoured to gain the *Habilitation* and it is evident that there were no hard feelings between them. When some of Edith's friends expressed the opinion that the professor had let her down, she would not hear of it. She wrote in response: 'one must keep reminding oneself that he himself suffers most because he has sacrificed his humanity to his science. That [work] is so overpowering and the amount of gratitude we owe him for it is so incalculable that, in view of that, any kind of personal resentment should not even arise. For me, he will always remain the Master, whose image cannot be blurred by any human weakness.' There was no more to be said!

There are considerable gaps in Edith's letters between 1922 and 1928. A letter of 1930 speaks of meeting him for the first time in eight years, the first occasion, in fact, since her conversion. She had an open and pleasurable conversation with him and one can well imagine how easily the old friends bridged the gap of those many years. For the celebration of his seventieth birthday in 1929, she wrote an essay, 'Husserl's Phenomenology and the Philosophy of Saint Thomas Aquinas'. She paid the Husserls a further and possibly a final visit in 1931 and mentions catching a late train home in order not to disturb 'the old folks'' afternoon nap.

Her entry to Carmel did not end the relationship and she remained in close touch by correspondence. How pleased the old man must have been to receive her letters. In January 1938 Edith was aware of his poor health and in March, while she was nursing a member of the Cologne community who lay dying, she realized her dear Master's time on earth was also drawing to a close. She often commended him to Sister Clara's prayers and wrote: 'I am not at all worried about my dear Master. It has always been far from me to think that God's mercy allows itself to be circumscribed by the visible church's boundaries.'

The Master died on 27 April, Good Friday, shortly after Edith's Perpetual Profession. She received a card from Frau Malvine confiding to her some of the professor's last words on Holy Thursday. Edith accepted this as a precious Profession gift and told a close friend that she had anticipated his death would come near her special day. This indicates what a close bond she had with her Master – second only to that with her mother?

She wrote to friends for news of his funeral and was saddened by a 'frighteningly icy report' in a Hamburg newspaper. She comforted herself by writing: 'That cannot harm the Master. He was detached from all that is mundane by the time he went home.'

Edith remained in contact with Frau Malvine up to the time of her deportation. The old lady lived to the age of ninety and became a Catholic.

During her years as student and assistant in Göttingen and Freiburg, Edith appeared to have no difficulty in adapting to life in a male-dominated world, where she found herself intellectually equal to the men. She absorbed Husserl's method of phenomenology, his meticulous analysis, with unwavering fidelity. There were two further streams of thought in the phenomenology of this period led by Scheler and (a few years later) Heidegger. Neither appealed to Edith as an alternative to Husserl's, nor did the later development of Husserl himself.

Her thesis, *On the Problem of Empathy*, was published in 1917, and further important works of hers appeared in Husserl's *Yearbook* in the 1920s. I am gratified, and find it 'very Edith', that she was able to maintain her phenomenological philosophy through and beyond her conversion, and ultimately to apply it to the spiritual.

CHAPTER SIX

A Restless Spirit

To follow Edith's footsteps between February 1918 and January 1922 is not easy. Her autobiography ends when she achieves her doctorate in 1916. Her letters between 1916 and 1920 provide only the occasional insights. There are no letters (available so far in English) between May 1920 and October 1922. Chronologies of her life suggest scientific work in Breslau 1919–1923 or freelance academic work 1918–1922 or in some cases there is no more than a blank. In Josephine Koeppel's comprehensive 'Chronology' which follows her translation of Edith's *Life*, she says, when referring to this period, 'Edith's personal spiritual journey preoccupied her for nearly three difficult years.' Yes, these were the years when her search for the truth began in earnest. Only Edith herself would know how painful a time it was.

After Edith left Freiburg, she wrote to a friend: 'I do not know yet what I should do were Husserl to take offence at my letter (of resignation) and if I were . . . to fall into disfavour. Perhaps I would go . . . to Göttingen where – if, indeed, anywhere – I would feel somewhat at home.' She sounds bereaved, anxious and uncertain. She expresses no resentment, and self-pity was unknown to her. However, she would hardly have been human had she not been both wounded and humbled. She was, after all, an ambitious twenty-five-year-old who had seemingly failed in her first assignment. She was about to do so again in the pursuit of her career as the Universities rejected her applications for *Habilitation*. Edith tells us she was not crushed. No, I cannot imagine a crushed Edith. But . . . she did not even admit to bruising. As I read her letters written two years later, I realized she had underplayed the significance of these two events. Maybe she did so to protect her Master, her frustrations and her own hidden deeper emotions.

Two years after the events, when no doubt her wounds had healed a little, her tone is different and this gives us the opportunity to share her true feelings. In defence of her friend, Hans Lipps, who also abandoned the Master, she writes: 'it was not nervousness that drove him away from Freiburg . . . I knew very well that he would not have enough emotional resistance to endure the skirmishes in *Lorettostrasse* [where Husserl lived] . . . he suffers unspeakably whenever confronted with *injustice* and there you run into that at every step.' It was quite different to defend a friend in this way, but defend herself she would not. It is likely she endured more than she ever admitted in Freiburg.

The second letter is one where she admits to initiating correspondence with the Universities on the injustice of women being denied *Habilitation*. She wrote to her friend: 'I am not thinking of trying again for *Habilitation*. That circular to the universities regarding the habilitation of women was due to my request, certainly, but I promise myself very little by way of results. It was only a rap on the knuckles for the gentlemen in Göttingen.' I am sure she felt all the better for having applied the rap!

In 1918 Edith was faced with 'herself' for the first time. Her carefully mapped life had run out of signposts. Where and what next must have been the questions which troubled her. For two years she was a rolling stone moving between Breslau, Göttingen and Freiburg. Her work alternated between Reinach's papers, Husserl's sixtieth-birthday *Festschrift* and her own attempts to gain *Habilitation*. The third option failed and the other two were completed. She returned to Breslau where she knew that her presence on a more permanent basis would please her mother. She had meanwhile achieved some philosophical work on her own account which she could continue at home. In a letter from Breslau, Edith wrote: '[for want of anything better] I have awarded myself [a licence to lecture] and am holding lectures with exercises in my home

. . . at which more than 30 people take part. Besides that I will soon begin [to teach] a course in the public high school on basic questions in ethics.' 'For want of anything better' suggests how little the idea appealed to her and how she was doing no more than marking time.

Inevitably, there were the usual family demands. To stay overnight with Aunt Bianca who was grieving over the loss of a daughter was not a difficult kindness to fulfil. Erna's problems were a different matter. I consider it a happy fault that in Chapter VI of her *Life*, Edith allows her memories to carry her well beyond the prescribed year of 1913. The chapter is given the title 'Two Young Hearts' but revolves around Erna rather more than herself. For this reason, she writes Erna's story to its natural conclusion when she is married in 1920. Had she not done so, we would have been denied the valuable insights into her own state of mind at this time. Erna's engagement to Hans Biberstein had been a protracted affair, and as arrangements for the marriage surfaced, there were anxieties over where she and Hans should live, where Hans should practise as a doctor and whether his mother should be invited to live with them. Throughout these troublesome times, Edith was both caring sister and wise counsellor. Erna and Hans were married in December 1920. Meanwhile, Edith shares her own anguish with us in the following way: 'I was passing through a personal crisis which was totally concealed from my relatives, one I was unable to resolve in our house.' By the time of the marriage, the strain began to tell and she writes again: 'my health was very poor, probably as a result of the spiritual conflicts I then endured in complete secrecy and without any human support.' Not for the first time Edith had given her undivided support for others with little regard for her own well-being.

A very happy letter was received from Erna on her honeymoon. This set Edith's mind at rest. '[A]nd I now,' she says, 'felt free to take care of myself.' How she was to do this, and exactly what her spiritual conflicts were, we are not told.

During this desert time it is likely Edith looked back and remembered how as a student she could not find time to investigate the questions of faith when they were presented to her by Max Scheler. How the lifestyle of many of her student friends, and indeed Reinach and to a lesser degree Husserl, reflected their Christianity. Reinach's philosophy was grounded in it and his wife Anna's faith had shone like a beacon in front of her very eyes. Perhaps she remembered the day Hans Lipps enquired if she was a member of the club which went to Mass every day and how, when she answered 'no', she almost added 'unfortunately'. She was already aware that her friends had something which she did not. A day spent in Frankfurt with Pauline Reinach in 1916 was another memory which was likely to come flooding back in her moments of thought and reflection. When visiting the Cathedral, Edith noticed a lady coming in with a shopping basket on her arm and settling into a pew as if for an intimate conversation. She believed you only went to synagogues and churches for services. That someone should enter for private prayer left a lasting impression. As did their visit to the Liebieg Institute where they saw a sculpture depicting Mary the Mother of God with John in the centre and with Magdalene and Nicodemus on either side. There was no image of Christ in the group, but it had a powerful influence on the two girls who, unbeknown to themselves, were already on their way to finding the image of Christ in their own lives. One wonders also if at times she pondered where her ambition and her scholarly achievements were leading her. In her darkest moments it must have seemed like up a blind alley.

When reading Edith's *Self-Portrait in Letters*, I became aware of her close friendship with Hedwig Conrad-Martius. It is she who provides the last and important link in this chapter. In her *Life*, Edith's references to Hedwig are tantalisingly few. Before she left for Göttingen in 1913, she saw a photograph of her in an illustrated journal. Hedwig had recently won a prize for a philosophical thesis and was remarked upon as 'Husserl's highly talented student'. Her marriage to Hans Theodor Conrad in 1912 is mentioned later, and we learn that they both taught philosophy in Munich and divided their time between this city and their home in the Palatine at Bergzabern. Hedwig received her doctorate in Munich and was a member of the Evangelical Church.

Edith wrote a letter in 1917 asking a friend to encourage Hedwig to visit them in Freiburg when the fruit had been safely harvested. This visit did not materialize. In 1918, Edith wrote a formal letter to Frau Dr Conrad concerning her work on Reinach's papers. It is apparent it was one of several written on the same subject. A footnote to this letter tells us Edith and Hedwig corresponded for two years before finally meeting in the summer of 1920.

The Bergzabern home of Hedwig and her husband Autós[1] was a gathering place, during their summer vacation, for members of the Göttingen Philosophy Circle. They met there in order to assist with the fruit harvest and to talk philosophy. It is surprising that Edith's first visit to Bergzabern was not made until the summer of 1920. And how the invitation came about then I have no idea.

Hedwig and Edith were acknowledged as two of Husserl's most gifted students. They were likely to have many things in common, not least their mutual respect for the Master. Their friendship soon blossomed, and I believe Edith had found the one she needed in her hour of need. Bergzabern offered a welcome respite from the stresses at Breslau and gave her the opportunity to think through, and maybe share, some of her personal problems. In the past, long hikes into the hills had often cleared Edith's mental cobwebs. The sweet-smelling orchards and gathering in the plum harvest must have had a similar therapeutic effect.

Hedwig's photo reveals a woman slightly older than Edith with a sweet and gentle countenance. It is likely she was soon aware of Edith's tensions. Religion was openly discussed at Bergzabern and Edith's own philosophical work was encouraged. She returned there again and again. Here she found the space and companionship which she craved as she slowly came to terms with the reality which she now faced ... And the reality was that she would sooner or later have to renounce atheism in favour of Christianity. During the years which followed her Freiburg experience, Edith was intent on finding the meaning to life itself. That she suffered an inner martyrdom as she relinquished herself to the guidance of the Holy Spirit – who was as yet unknown to her – is certain. In her essay, 'Plant Soul, Animal Soul, Human Soul', it was considered by some that she had already accepted the Christian faith. And yet she remained unable to take that final step. Whether there remained a small seed of doubt, or whether her mother's

---

[1]Autós was the nickname of Hans Theodor Conrad.

likely hurt and anguish had to be fully reconciled in her heart
first, we shall never know.

Hedwig became Edith's 'dear Hatti', and as they shared her
extended stay at Bergzabern in 1921, Hatti remembers Edith
as intensely quiet. 'It was,' she said, 'as if we were both
walking on a narrow mountain ridge, aware that God's call
was imminent.'[2] It is apparent to me that while Hatti was
already a believer, she was deeply aware of Edith's personal
struggle and that she accompanied and sustained her in a
special way throughout the final weeks towards conversion.

One evening, Edith was left on her own, and taking a book
from the shelves at random, she sat down ready for a good
read. The book was none other than St Teresa of Avila's *Book
of Her Life* in which Teresa in her own colourful language
shares her faith and absolute trust in her loving Saviour. Edith
did not put the book down until the last page was turned. Her
search was over. '*Das ist die Wahrheit.*' She now knew: 'That
is the Truth.'

It was fitting that Edith's baptism should take place in the
Catholic Church of Bergzabern and that Hatti should be her
godmother. Together they had provided the safe harbour
which Edith sought as she came to the end of her first great
spiritual journey. Hatti remained Edith's staunch and dearest
friend until the end of her life.

---

[2]Freda Mary Oben, *Edith Stein. Scholar, Feminist, Saint*, New York, Alba House
(Society of St Paul), 1988, p.17.

Auguste Stein c. 1920s.

Below: Edith 'the tot', taken from a family group picture.

Above: The sisters Erna and Edith c. 1898.

Edith the student at Breslau
1913–1914.

Professor Edmund Husserl,
'The Master'.

Above: Adolf and Anna Reinach,
close friends in Göttingen.

Left: Edith in 1921.

The sculpture of the Mourning Group at the Liebieg Institute, Frankfurt.

Left: Hedwig Conrad-Martius, 'dear Hatti', at work in the Bergzabern orchard.

Right: The font in the Catholic church of Bergzabern where Edith was baptised on 1 January 1921.

Three photographs of Edith between
1923–1931, her years at St Magdalena's.

Above Right: Canon Joseph Schwind, Vicar General of Speyer.

Above Left: Beuron Abbey, viewed from beneath the Holzbrücke, the wooden bridge across the Danube.

Right: Archabbot Raphael Walzer of Beuron, Edith's spiritual director 1928–1933.

Rosa Stein in the 1920s.

Mother Petra Brüning,
Superior of the Ursuline
Convent, Dorsten.

Ruth Kantorowicz.

Sister Teresia Renata de Spiritu Sancto, Edith's novice mistress, Superior and biographer.

Edith, the Carmelite Novice.

Left: Edith at Echt Carmel 1941.

Right: Edith and Rosa at Echt, July 1939.

Station Master Fouquet.

Der Zug, mit dem auch die Jüdin,
Philosophin und Karmelitin

EDITH STEIN

nach Auschwitz deportiert wurde,
hielt am 7. August 1942 gegen 13 Uhr
kurz auf Gleis 3 dieses Bahnhofs.
Von hier kam
ihr letztes Lebenszeichen.

The memorial plaque at Schifferstadt station.

CHAPTER SEVEN

A New Life

Many a time I have been an uninvited guest at St Martin's Church in Bergzabern. I stand unobserved in a corner from where I have a good view of the handsome stone font around which I see a group, a very small group of people. It is New Year's Day 1922 and the parish priest, Dean Breitling, is presiding over a carefully prepared Baptismal Liturgy. It is after all no everyday occurrence to receive a noted philosopher and Jewess, Dr Edith Stein, into the Catholic Church. Edith's slim eager figure is joined by the shorter but reassuring person of her chosen godmother, the staunch Lutheran and dear friend Hatti. I believe I see a shadow of Autós, Hatti's husband, and I hear the Dean proclaim Edith's Baptismal names, Teresa Hedwig, as he bathes her head with Holy Water and welcomes her as a member of the Catholic Church. A lump comes into my throat as I gaze at the thirty-year-old who has struggled so long to find the truth and who from now on will subject her life to this truth. The strong will, the high intelligence, the ambition and the independence are placed irrevocably in God's hands.

Dean Breitling was surprised when, a few weeks earlier, Edith arrived in his sacristy and asked for Baptism. He soon discovered she had prepared herself carefully with the aid of a catechism, a missal and daily attendance at Mass. He may have been equally surprised at her request that Hatti, a Lutheran, should stand as her godmother. The Dean was a discerning man who was able to treat this unusual situation with the wisdom it required. In a letter to the Dean, Edith signs herself 'With most respectful greetings, your ever grateful Edith Stein' and some years later she refers to him affectionately as her 'old pastor'.

Arrangements were made for Edith to be confirmed by the Bishop of Speyer in the Cathedral on 2 February, the Feast of Candlemas. It is more than likely this was when she met Canon Schwind, Vicar General of the Diocese of Speyer, who was to be her trusted friend and spiritual guide for some years to come. Hatti tells us Edith's joy at this time was 'childlike'. And yet there were so few with whom she could share this joy. A visit to Breslau to tell her mother and the family her news could be delayed no longer. It required all her courage to face the pain she knew it would cause.

As she knelt at her mother's feet she looked straight into her eyes and said, 'Mother, I am a Catholic'. She hardly expected the response she received . . . tears gushed from the eyes of the mother she loved so well, the mother whom she had never seen shed a tear before. Edith wept with her. In order to reassure her and the rest of the family of her continued love and concern for them she remained in Breslau for six months. Daily Mass had become an essential part of life. She attended the early morning one at St Michael's, rising while the rest of the family slept in order to avoid disturbing the rhythm of the household. Occasionally she accompanied her mother to the Synagogue and the old lady became aware of her daughter's strength of prayer. While the family could not understand her conversion they discovered a 'new' Edith but realized her bond with them remained as strong as ever.

Almost immediately after her conversion Edith felt drawn to the religious life, believing this was the only way of leading a truly devout life in God's service. Canon Schwind advised her against this and introduced her to the Dominican Sisters in Speyer where she accepted a teaching position which she held for eight years. During this time she grew in her discovery of God, in a deepening prayer life and in the knowledge that a Christian life is one which accepts that everything comes from the hand of God. She was given a small room at the cloister gate and adopted a very simple lifestyle. She joined the Sisters for Daily Mass and the Divine Office and spent many hours in private prayer. She was frugal in her dress and eating-habits. As well as teaching in the school she was invited to coach the Dominican novices in Latin but was not, as is sometimes suggested, their novice mistress. In 1925 she wrote to Fritz Kaufmann: 'For all of three years now I have been living behind the sheltering walls of a convent, at heart – and this I may surely say without any presumption – like a real nun, even though I wear no veil and am not bound by vows or enclosure.'

An aerial view of St Magdalena's shows an impressive complex of buildings, a small township in its own right. The Dominican Sisters were responsible for a secondary school and a college for teacher training and pedagogy. Mother Ambrosia, Prioress for twenty-five years, had an astonishing community of one hundred and seventy-nine sisters in her care when Edith joined them, of whom one hundred and twenty were choir nuns and the remainder lay sisters. While St Magdalena's lay in the shadow of Speyer's Imperial Cathedral, it, not surprisingly, had its own elegant church which was consecrated as early as 1718. Up to one hundred students were accommodated at any one time and future women teachers were educated alongside the postulant nuns. The monastery had its own extensive grounds, garden and vineyard. It was into this secluded world of 'its own' that Edith accepted a teaching post in 1923 with German and history her appointed subjects. For the first time in her life she settled contentedly to her task. I say this because earlier in her career it was easy to tell she had no great love of teaching and it was not her chosen vocation. On more than one occasion in the past she had taught 'for want of anything better'. She once wrote to a friend after she had completed a period of teaching: 'the spectre of a return to teaching has been banished, and that is a great relief.' A Dominican Sister of Speyer recalled that teaching for Edith was not a labour of love but rather a duty. She was not, she said, sustained or enthused by teaching. In another letter Edith writes: 'I do not take myself too seriously as a teacher and still have to smile when I have to put it down anywhere as my profession.'

Edith's earlier attitude to teaching did not affect her work at St Magdalena's where she was devoted and diligent and became a caring and respected educator. She was said to be both painstaking and strict. She influenced those she taught by who she was, a tranquil and dignified person who was generous with her free time and who took the students on excursions to the theatre – she introduced them to Shakespeare – to farms and other outside activities. The nineteen-year-old students welcomed her company for philosophical discussions and song-singing. She made good friends among the religious community and was known to join the lay sisters to wash the dishes after meals. Edith embraced life fully at St Magdalena's and she was held in warm affection.

Two of the Dominican Sisters of Speyer became Edith's particular friends, Sr Callista and Sr Agnella. I imagine they were students in her Latin class as novices and when they moved away from Speyer, the mother house, for further studies in Munich or to teach in Ludwigshafen, they wrote to Edith seeking her advice on both spiritual matters and teaching methods. They shared their anxieties and concerns with her and she responded with sound practical advice. Letters flowed between them from 1927 until 1942. Sr Callista wrote to Edith on the occasion of Canon Schwind's death and Edith replied: 'I know there is no one in St Magdalena['s] who more truly shares my joys and sorrows than you.' She continues with the following advice concerning Sr Agnella: 'She bears a cross like everyone else, but it has borne fruit for her . . . We too . . . have to learn to see that others have a cross to carry and to realize we cannot take it from them. It is harder than carrying one's own, but it cannot be avoided.'

A letter written to Sr Agnella from Echt in 1939 contains a treatise, a little gem, in reply to a question from Sister on how to balance Christian freedom and at the same time fulfil monastic prescriptions. Edith writes: 'Our holy Rule and Constitutions are for us the expression of the Divine will. To sacrifice personal inclinations for their sake is to participate in the sacrifice of Christ . . . I believe that you yourself have already found an answer in your 'being a root' – an image to be understood [with a grain of salt] because, after all, we are not a grapevine, but simply branches. Our roots are in the heart of Jesus.' How gently she guides this Sister along the right path.

Canon Schwind was Edith's dear friend and spiritual adviser for the first four and a half years of her life at St Magdalena's. He welcomed her at his home each Sunday afternoon when they shared a cup of coffee and deep theological discussions. After she left, the good canon joined his niece Anna (who was his housekeeper) and, sinking into an armchair, he exclaimed: 'Oh, this philosopher! She can ask more questions than could be answered by ten learned theologians.'[1] In September 1927, Canon Schwind collapsed while in the confessional. By the time Edith reached him he was dead. She spent the entire night beside his body praying. His death was a deep personal loss for her. In an obituary which she wrote for the *Innsbruck Review*, we learn how well she had come to know and respect this holy man. A short quotation gives a taste of her understanding of him: 'Strict and kind, serious and gay, dignified and humble, his soul brought these many contrasting shades of character into harmony because they reflected his pure love for God.'[2]

Edith's friendship with the Schwind family did not die with the canon. It gave her great pleasure to have one of his nieces present at her clothing ceremony in April 1934.

Before he died, the canon introduced Edith to the Jesuit priest, Father Erich Przywara, a noted philosopher of theology. Father Erich remembers their first meeting in the following words: 'So we had our first conversation in Speyer, under the auspices of the unforgettable, wise and kindly Vicar-General Dr Schwind. Dr Schwind told me at once that I was going to have a surprise: for he had never met anyone whose looks betrayed her race as little as those of Edith Stein . . . This was indeed a very special trait of Edith Stein – she came from absolutely pure Jewish blood and was yet a true German woman . . . From this sprang the really great style of Edith Stein: classical, philosophical austerity . . . and deeply artistic feeling.'[3]

I have the impression that Edith's relationship with Father Erich Przywara was more formal than that which she had enjoyed with the canon. Whether this was so or not, it was Father Erich's wise counsel which directed her forward, beyond her life as a teacher and beyond her very private

---

[1] *Kölner Selig-und Heiligsprechungsprozeß der Dienerin Gottes Sr Teresia Benedicta a Cruce*, 1962, Art. 115, pp. 35–37.
[2] Sister Teresia de Spiritu Sancto, ODC, *Edith Stein*, trs. Cecil Hastings and Donald Nicholl, London & New York: Sheed and Ward, 1952, p.81.
[3] Hilda C Graef, *The Scholar and the Cross. The Life and Work of Edith Stein*, London, New York & Toronto, Longmans, 1955, p.48.

prayer life within the Dominican family. He realized that the absence of any scholarly work in her daily routine was denying if not wasting her academic ability. It was he who commissioned Edith to translate John Henry Newman's *Letters and Diaries* from English into German. And later the more testing assignment of translating St Thomas Aquinas' *Quaestiones Disputatae de Veritate* from Latin into German. This was published in her home town of Breslau in two volumes in 1932. It is described as a unique translation in which Edith employs her phenomenological skills to interpret the Thomistic doctrine.

It was also Father Erich's suggestion that she write *Life in a Jewish Family* and that she visit the Abbey of Beuron to gain a wider perspective of the Catholic Church. His guidance had a compelling influence on the direction of Edith's life but he may not have foreseen that it would culminate in Carmel. He visited her at Cologne on one occasion, and in two of her last letters to friends, written from Echt, she enquires of his health, which indicates they had not kept in touch.

Edith visited the Benedictine Abbey of Beuron for the first time for Holy Week and Easter in 1928. Beuron was a noted centre for the Arts and Liturgical Renewal and the Liturgical movement was developing even as Edith became a regular visitor. Here she enjoyed the rich monastic Benedictine Liturgy and at the same time discovered a perfect soul mate in the Archabbot of the Monastery, Raphael Walzer. He was a younger man than the canon but was very alive to Edith's many gifts. He wrote of her: 'I have seldom met a soul which united so many excellent qualities; and she was simplicity and naturalness personified ... She was simple with simple people, learned with the learned yet without presumption, an enquirer with enquirers, and I would almost like to add, a sinner with sinners.'[4]

Edith's biographer and novice mistress, Sr Teresia de Spiritu Sancto, tells us that Edith was able to share her innermost thoughts with Abbot Raphael and that she looked upon herself as his spiritual daughter. The canon had been a father figure and she his daughter but I sense an indefinable difference between the two relationships. Beuron became her spiri-

---

[4]Sister Teresia de Spiritu Sancto, op.cit., p. 83.

tual home, a haven which she visited as often as possible. She trusted Abbot Raphael and accepted his advice on deferring her desire for religious life.

Beuron is an imposing abbey situated in the upper valley of the Danube, a truly idyllic setting. To reach it you walk across an ancient, majestic, covered wooden bridge which spans the Danube. As I did so, one September day in 1987, I visualized the many times Edith had done so, in the early hours of a March or April morning as the sun was rising through the mist beyond the Abbey. She was on her way to the monastery church and the place in which she chose to pray before a portrait of Our Lady of Sorrows. She stayed in a small guest-house beside the bridge where she received warm hospitality from the Mayer family. On 9 April 1928 she signed their visitors' book with the words: 'In the hope that very soon I shall again be able to go from the hospitable home at the Holzbrücke [the wooden bridge] to the "House of the Lord," and with sincere gratitude.' She became a very regular visitor during the next five years.

It was her custom to arrive at the abbey in time to commence a private retreat from Palm Sunday in preparation for the Easter Liturgy. During this week she did not write letters or converse and we may be sure fasting accompanied these disciplines which she imposed on herself. This time was given entirely to her Lord and Heavenly Master; to accompany Him step by step throughout His Passion was her choice and privilege. On Good Friday she spent many hours kneeling in an upright position and lesser mortals marvelled at her strength of endurance, though Edith herself would hardly have used such a word. Perhaps it was not so surprising that Edith who had always 'observed' the Day of Atonement, who was herself a child of this day, was so perfectly able to share it with her Saviour. In her *Prayer of the Church* Edith reminds us that the Day of Atonement is the Old Testament antecedent of Good Friday. Did not her mother spend many similar hours of prayer in the Synagogue on this very day?

From Beuron Edith received a treasure which she said she kept for a very long time. After an Easter visit she wrote: 'these most blessed days cannot be expressed in speech, much less in writing.' In 1932 she reflects on whether her frequent visits there can be justified but concludes: 'one has to provide one's inner life with the nourishment it needs, especially when at other times we are required to give a great deal to others.' Yes, Beuron became a fountain from which she could slake her thirst. Some of her friends thought she might well fulfil her wish for religious life by joining the Benedictines, but no – it was always Carmel for which Edith thirsted.

As I scanned the many letters Edith wrote while teaching at Speyer, I was searching for clues about her own life. Instead, I found little about herself, her concern being for the problem or anxiety facing the recipient of the letter. One set of correspondence with a difference was that to Sr Adelgundis OSB. Fifty-one letters were written between 1930 and 1938 and reveal an interesting relationship. Sister was a student of Husserl's and was in Edith's 'Kindergarten' at Freiburg. She became a Catholic and joined the Benedictine Sisters of St Lioba in Freiburg-Günterstal. Edith had another friend in this community, Sr Placida, and she often visited St Lioba's. Her correspondence with Sr Adelgundis is of a different nature from that written to the Dominican Sisters. Here she is writing to a former philosophy colleague who remains in close touch with the Husserls and who is also a religious. Sister provides a bridge between the old and the new, and prior to Edith's entry to Carmel their correspondence is brisk and covers many areas. On more than one occasion, Sister criticizes Edith's lectures. The first time it is accepted as justified and no offence is taken. On the second occasion Edith writes: 'But then, it appears that you did not want the supernatural to be brought up at all. But, if I could not speak about that, I probably would not mount a lecturer's platform at all.' She confides in Sister when she feels the time is coming to leave St Magdalena's and she shares her family problems and concerns about her own workload.

The closeness of this relationship appears to decline after Edith enters Carmel, only one letter a year in four years. Sister visited her in Cologne when in urgent need of advice. Edith had to leave the parlour before their discussion was completed and this pained her greatly. In another letter, Sister Adelgundis mentions how she dislikes the Carmelite custom (of those days) of lowering the veil over the face when in the parlour with visitors. Sister was obviously a strong-minded character not afraid to speak her mind. She remained in touch with Edith until after Husserl's death but there are no further letters in print beyond this. She was Husserl's spiritual friend throughout his illness and was with him when he died.

In March 1931 Edith wrote to Sr Callista from Beuron: 'on Thursday I took leave of St Magdalena's. St Thomas [her translation] is no longer satisfied with my spare time, he demands all of me.' To Fritz Kaufmann she writes: 'Since I found it impossible to keep up with all the urgent duties, I finally felt compelled to leave St Magdalena's . . . The good sisters were very loath to let me go, and did so only because they saw [Father Przywara].'

From Breslau she wrote to Sr Adelgundis, 'When I decided to leave Speyer, I knew it would be very difficult not to be living in a convent any longer. But I would never have imagined that it would be as difficult as it has proved to be in these first months. For all that, as I cannot doubt that things are as they should be, I have never for a moment regretted making the move.'

In Edith's fragmented life, eight years was a long time to have spent in one place. By now she had in many ways 'outgrown' Speyer. She was no longer the new convert but someone fully – more fully than most – versed in the theology and life of the Church. Her years of teaching had given her the experience and authority to speak publicly on education. She realized she had become too heavily burdened with teaching, academic work and lecturing. The time had come to say goodbye to teaching and to pick up the challenge of another new start.

CHAPTER EIGHT

Dr Stein – Lecturer

When Edith arrived at St Magdalena's in 1923 she adopted her usual single-minded approach. She was there for two reasons, to nurture her Christian faith and to tutor her students. Further philosophical work did not belong in her new life – or so she believed – and it was foregone. Her desire for Carmel was never far away but she respected those who told her the time was not yet ripe. It was not until she met St Thomas Aquinas in her translation of his work that she understood you could pursue learning in the service of God and only then, she tells us, could she bring herself to take up serious intellectual work again.

We cannot be sure when news of her name as an educator first seeped beyond the walls of St Magdalena's to the provincial town of Speyer. Once it had, Edith received invitations to share her views on education in public. Some of her earlier philosophical work was at the same time published in Husserl's *Year Book*. Slowly but surely the Catholic world became aware of Dr Stein, recently converted to the Catholic Church, living and teaching behind the sheltering walls of St Magdalena's. She received invitations to lecture from across Germany and beyond. Twenty years earlier she had been awarded her doctorate *summa cum laude* and only now did she have the opportunity to fulfil all her early promise. Edith was a natural speaker who captivated her listeners and who was by this time so totally given to God that she was working through Him and for Him.

Dr Lucy Gelber writes: 'As a speaker, she appeared on the platform without fear but also without vanity to serve the cause of religious education with electrifying eloquence. She left the speaker's stand without being carried away by the applause of the audience or by the enjoyment of a personal success.'[1]

As time passed, Edith was acknowledged to be a leading intellectual Catholic feminist of the day. I hesitated before introducing this comment for fear it raised the spectre of strident demands for equality of the sexes. Nothing could have been further from Edith's message. As a student at Breslau University she admitted to radical feminism until, she says, she became tired of it. Now it was her task to express her views on the vocation and value of women in national life – *not* radically, but objectively, applying the Catholic viewpoint. That she did so with great effect there is little doubt.

One of Edith's early lectures was given to an association of women teachers at Ludwigshafen on the Rhine in April 1928. This was the signal for her invitations to mushroom and she soon found herself with an onerous workload. Her friend, Sr Callista, wrote to her suggesting she had now 'become' someone. Edith assures her this is not so: 'It does appear as though the orbit of my daily duties is to expand. But that, in my opinion, does not change anything about me. It has been demanded of me, and I have undertaken it.' It was as if she had been catapulted into a situation, not of her own making but one which she could not bypass. Her life was taking on a new texture, moving out of seclusion into the limelight. Sr Callista need not have feared. Edith's essential, deep inner core of commitment to her God was unlikely to be shaken by public acclaim.

The archive manuscripts of Edith's lectures reveal how painstakingly these were prepared. Our Lady, Mary, was used as her role-model for many of them. Mary's *fiat*, Bethlehem, Nazareth, and Mary at the heart of the first Christian community, were images used for her famous Salzburg address. This, *The Ethos of Women's Professions*, was given on 1 September

---

[1]From the 'Editors' Introduction To the First Edition', in Edith Stein, *Essays on Woman*, 2nd ed. revised, tr. Freda Mary Oben, Washington, ICS Publications (The Collected Works of Edith Stein, vol. 2), 1996, p.5.

1930 at the Association of Catholic Academics. Following the lecture Edith wrote: 'Salzburg has drawn astonishing ripples. I have to show up as a speaker here, there, and everywhere. In between, there are mountains of essays [to be corrected].'

Dr Vierneisel, a Professor of Philosopher from Heidelberg, contributed a long and complimentary review of her lecture to the October issue of the *Heidelberg Bote*. It is well summarized in his final paragraph: 'Edith Stein's lecture was most convincing because it was free of the pathos of the *feminist movement* and because the speaker herself markedly and visibly personified her own thoughts. Her bearing when she descended from the podium recalled those paintings in which ancient masters depicted Mary's visit to the temple.'[2]

Yes, Salzburg was the catalyst and six months later, Edith was preparing to leave St Magdalena's. Before doing so she was encouraged to seek *Habilitation* once more. Both Freiburg and Breslau Universities presented possibilities, but neither materialized. Edith was well used to such rejections. They did not trouble her. On leaving Speyer, Edith went home to Breslau for a prolonged stay of seven months. From there she could continue work on her own 'big project', *Potentiality and Act*, and at the same time fulfil her lecture engagements. Her sister Rosa was in special need of her presence, a further incentive for her decision.

This is Edith's life and for that reason there have been few references to her siblings and none at all yet to Rosa, her senior by eight years. It is fair to say that Rosa spent the middle and final years of her life in Edith's shadow. We are often told how they shared the last terrible journey to Auschwitz but what more do we know of Rosa? As I try to piece together what will necessarily be a subjective sketch of Rosa, I take a long look at the two photographs I have of her. The first is a small portrait of a youthful Rosa which shows exceptionally fine features. She has Edith's deep-set eyes, no cleft in her chin, and dark hair in natural waves above her brow. The second is the one more often used and shows her standing beside Edith; it was taken at Echt in 1939. She would have been fifty-eight years old and is wearing a polka-dot

---

[2] Quoted in Lucy Gelber, 'Editors' Introduction To the First Edition', in Edith Stein, *Essays on Woman*, op.cit., p.23.

wrapover pinafore with her strong working hands clasped in front of her. The pinafore was a symbol of her trade, that of housekeeper, and the fact she did not remove it for the photograph indicates she felt very much at home in it. Her hair was white by this time, parted in the middle and drawn back severely.

Rosa was the odd one out in the Stein family of seven children. Her destiny was not to follow a career as had the rest, nor yet to consider marriage which she disdained, but instead to oversee the running of the family home at 39, Michaelis-strasse. In Chapter III of Edith's *Life* I learned that Rosa was a tomboy as a teenager, with no inclination for learning or study. Auguste was concerned for her future and sent her to some aunts to be trained as a housekeeper. This was a happy time for her, but to take up the reins of the family household in Breslau was, I believe, no easy task. There was a constantly moving population with family, extended family and friends passing through the ever open door. Many of her duties were shared with her elder sister, Frieda, with whom she never had a happy relationship. Was there a lack of fulfilment and contentment in Rosa's life which bred an element of resentment? Her sharp tongue greatly grieved Auguste, and Edith was often called upon to calm troubled waters when she was at home. Was it because Edith was so good a mediator that the sisters – so very different in temperament – became closer? Did Rosa share her frustrations with Edith and Edith her inner contentment, the fruit of her conversion, with Rosa? Did Rosa have a gap in her life just waiting to be filled with that same peace? We do not know when or how Rosa experienced her conversion but by the time of Edith's prolonged visit in 1931, both she and Edith knew her future lay within the Catholic Church. At the same time, they realized what a cruel blow it would be for their mother to lose a second daughter to Christianity. Auguste's business and her own physical powers were failing. They determined to do all they could to protect her from further pain. Rosa waited in patient self-sacrifice until her mother's death in 1936.

While Edith's months at home were a source of solace and support for Rosa, they were hard times for herself. She was accustomed to living under the same roof as the Blessed Sacrament, to being able to join the Sisters for the liturgy, and to enjoying the company of people who shared her spirituality. All this was now denied her. She and Rosa were able to creep out of the house undetected in the early hours of each morning to hear Mass at half past five at St Michael's Church. This apart, Edith writes of 'silent liturgy' as her 'portion' but maintains that '[e]ven in this way one can be richly supplied'.

Edith dedicated her time in Breslau – at the expense of all else, even letter-writing – to her own philosophical work. When apologising to Fritz Kaufmann for a long silence, she writes: 'I have other ways and means of keeping the bonds [of friendship] alive.' Prayer had indeed become a way of life for her.

In May 1931 she was invited to Vienna to give a talk on St Elisabeth of Thuringia, a popular saint, the 700th anniversary of whose death was being honoured. Edith celebrated this event at various venues on no fewer than eleven occasions. The Vienna appointment provided an excuse to 'flee' (from Breslau) in time for the feast of Pentecost, which she spent with the Steyler Missionaries in Mödling. Train timetables and convent hospitality guides were Edith's constant companions throughout her months on the lecture circuit.

By the middle of October, it was time for her to move on. Her diary was crammed with appointments in Aachen, Munich, Bonn and elsewhere. It was possible for her to spend a few days at Speyer, Advent at St Lioba's in Freiburg and Christmas, for the second year running, at Beuron. She was finding the constant travel tiring and after a series of lectures in Zürich in January 1932, her future was uncertain. She asked Sr Callista 'to implore the Christ Child to let me know what he intends to do with me'. These prayers were answered by an interview in February at the Münster Institute for Scientific Pedagogy where she was offered a post. She took up residence at the Collegium Marianum, which housed women students, and was faced with the challenge of an entirely new sphere of endeavour.

It has not been easy to unravel the web of Edith's life for the sixteen months or so she spent at Münster. She was in her forty-first year when she arrived and had been out of the mainstream academic world for so long that, as she tells a friend, she had to put up a struggle to justify her scholarly existence. She may have set herself apart from the rest of the staff by choosing to join the students for meals. And by her own natural reserve and austere way of life. That she soon found her way into the hearts of her students there is little doubt. She often joined them for their parties and was invited to the student union for a Christmas celebration of St Nicholas. It was held on 8 December, the feast of the Immaculate Conception. After St Nicholas' visit, which one of the students performed, they sat down to a plate and a glass of punch. Beside each plate was a holy picture of Our Lady. It was an important feast which Edith determined should not be overlooked.

In three long letters written to 'dear Hatti' between November 1932 and April 1933, Edith bares her soul. She is losing all confidence in herself and writes of having lost connection and of being generally incompetent for this world. She feared she was overreaching her capabilities in the philosophical work she had undertaken and even writes of her poor memory and ignorance. Can this be the Edith on whose words so many lingered? As I read the high opinion of members of the Münster staff, I conclude it was Edith's personal dilemma. She was not reaching her own high standards rather than anything more serious. She contributed two major lecture courses during her time at the Institute, on the 'Problems of Contemporary Girls' Education' and 'The Structure of the Human Person' but ... they cost her more time and effort than she considered reasonable. What a sharp critic of herself she was.

Maria Schmitz, cofounder of the Institute which appointed Edith, wrote: 'She distinguishes herself through her great piety and the very deep religiosity of her whole being. She is really a good interior soul, which is accompanied by an untiring diligence in her professional work.'[3] The librarian at the Institute – who saw Edith with great regularity – had a similar high regard for her and said: 'She stood head and shoulders above the other tutors on account of her intense thought, her broad culture, her masterly exposition and her capacity for recollection amidst many distractions.'[4]

---

[3]From the *Testimony of the Parish Office of Our Lady – Überwasser, Münster in Westphalia, 13 June 1933*, quoted in Marco Paolinelli, OCD et al., *Santa Teresa Benedetta della Croce (Edith Stein)*, Arenzano (GE), Carmelitani Scalzi, 1998, p.30.
[4]Sister Teresia de Spiritu Sancto, op.cit., p.113.

There are a handful of high points in Edith's life which provide me with a vivid picture and a sense of having 'been' there. 12 September 1932 at Juvisy near Paris is one of them. Edith was invited by the Société Thomiste to attend a conference on Phenomenology and Thomism. This was a rare opportunity for Edith who made it an excuse to see something of Paris and to stay with an old friend from her days at Göttingen, Professor Alexander Koyré. En route she visited Hatti, who was in hospital in Heidelberg, and the Benedictine Abbey at Neuburg. Alexander Koyré – Professor of Philosophy at the École des Hautes Études – was a friend for whom Edith had a profound respect, and I feel sure this was reciprocated. I notice he visited Edith in Münster on one occasion and at Cologne Carmel on another.

The paper at Juvisy on the Phenomenological Movement was given by Daniel Feuling OSB but it was Edith – the only woman present – who took all the questions in the discussion which followed. She was, after all, on her 'own ground' and no doubt her invitation was sent for this reason. All those years of pleasure and pain with the Master, all those hours as a 'neophyte in scholasticism . . . an unsuspecting little David [attacking] Goliath' as she translated St Thomas, culminated at Juvisy, one woman among thirty-five men, luminous and authentic. After the conference, Professor Rosenmöller wrote: 'The discussion was dominated entirely by Edith Stein. Certainly she had the best understanding of Husserl, having been for years his assistant in Freiburg, but she developed her thoughts with such clarity, in French when necessary, that she made an extraordinarily strong impression on this learned company of scholars.'[5]

Professor Rosenmöller was also from Münster and both he and his family became Edith's personal friends. It was the habit in the philosophical circles of those times for the lively academics to meet on a Sunday afternoon in the front room of one house or another. The Rosenmöllers played host to such a group which Edith joined. They were a Catholic family who detested anti-Semitism. Bernhard Rosenmöller was Professor of Religious Philosophy at the Münster Institute. Among other things, he edited their quarterly journal and was strongly

---

[5]Oben, op.cit., p.25.

influenced by phenomenology. It is not too surprising, then, that Edith was at home with this family. She went on a weekend retreat with the professor's wife and was a particular favourite with their youngest son, Anselm. When he was ordained priest in 1957, twenty-five years later, he used Edith's photo on his souvenir holy card. He acknowledged her saintliness before the Church and the rest of us! The professor attended Edith's clothing ceremony at Cologne Carmel and when the family moved to Breslau in 1937 they kept a caring eye on Rosa, whom they found to be reserved, shy almost, but very considerate. The professor's eldest son writes in his memoir of the Steins: 'I myself always turn with my concerns to both sisters at once, they belong together, not only in their dying, but probably also for all eternity.'[6]

Edith spent Christmas 1932 at the Ursuline Convent of Dorsten. Two of their sisters were staying at the Marianum and they asked their superior, Mother Petra Brüning, to extend the invitation. From her first meeting with Mother Petra, Edith knew it was a friendship, a kinship, unlike any other. She writes of a strong inner bond which grew and endured until the end of her life. After she entered Carmel, it was as if they shared their religious and prayer life, together and yet apart. Her thirty-two letters, all, save two, written from Carmel, are transparent and reveal a hint of dependence on Mother Petra's understanding and motherly goodness.

Invitations to lecture beyond her work at the Institute continued to arrive and Edith did not spare herself travelling to Essen, Augsburg, Ludwigshafen (for the second or third time) and to Munich where she gave a series of talks on Bavarian Radio.

During her time at Münster, Edith was more aware than most of the threat that the rise of National Socialism posed for both Germany and the Jewish people. On 30 January 1933, Hitler became Chancellor of Germany and on 27 February the *Reichstag* was burned to the ground and the Third Reich was established immediately thereafter. Jews were being relieved of public duties especially in the world of education. By

---

[6]Bernhard Rosenmöller, Jr., 'Edith Stein and the Family of the Religious Philosopher Bernhard Rosenmöller', in Waltraud Herbstrith, OCD (ed.), *Never Forget. Christian and Jewish Perspectives on Edith Stein*, tr. Susanne Batzdorff, Washington, ICS Publications, 1998 (pp.241–245), p.245.

1 April, an anti-Jewish boycott was put into effect throughout Germany and members of her family were affected. Edith felt unable to stand by and do nothing. She tried in vain to arrange a private audience with the Pope in order to persuade him to write an encyclical to alert the world of the imminent dangers. A letter with this request was delivered to Rome by hand by Abbot Raphael but Edith received no more than an acknowledgement and a blessing for her family. She gave her last lecture at the Institute on 25 February but remained on the staff doing private work until the end of June.

Her German and Jewish roots were both strong and precious to her and it was a painful time as she began to look forward to an uncertain future for her country, her people and herself.

This phase of Edith's life was a confusion of shades and colours, of endless travel, of spent energy, of fruition, of hidden anxieties and constant prayer. She had been obedient to Abbot Raphael's counsel and shared her knowledge of education and her understanding of the intrinsic value of women to the Catholic world in Germany. Her task was done. Had it not been, would Edith Stein ever have reached the Church history books?

CHAPTER NINE

Carmel at Last

When Edith returned to Münster after her Easter retreat at Beuron she found the Institute in turmoil and its entire future uncertain. She saw quite clearly that her employment there would soon end. At the same time she realized her days of influence as a speaker were over. The time had come when her entry to Carmel need no longer be delayed. Surely her mother would prefer to have her living in a convent in Germany rather than in South America where she had been offered a teaching post?

On 30 April – Good Shepherd Sunday – St Ludger's church celebrated its patronal feast with thirteen hours of prayer. Edith determined to be there and to ask the Good Shepherd for an answer to her question – could she now enter Carmel? As the final blessing was given she received His consent. All she now required was the blessing of her temporal shepherd, Abbot Raphael. This was gladly given.

Edith had two contacts in Cologne. Hedwig Spiegel, a Jewish friend who was her catechumen and with whom she had recently visited the Carmelite chapel for an hour of prayer. And Dr Cosack, a Catholic teacher whom she had met in Aachen and who had close connections with the Carmel. It was to her that Edith turned for an introduction to the Prioress of Cologne Carmel.

In 1933 the Carmel of Our Lady of Peace had a full complement of sisters, twenty, but was planning a new foundation in Edith's home town of Breslau. Three sisters were preparing to move from Cologne to Breslau, thus leaving room for new postulants. As so often in Edith's life we see the finger of God's hand in each phase of her journey. Cologne Carmel did, I believe, with a certain amount of hindsight, provide the right environment for so gifted and unusual a candidate to the Carmelite life.

Edith's first meeting was with the Prioress, Mother Josepha of the Blessed Sacrament, and the Novice Mistress, Mother Teresia Renata de Spiritu Sancto, from now on referred to as Mother Renata.[1] She was asked to give an account of herself and her spiritual journey since her conversion. The sisters were not concerned that she was Jewish, forty-two years old and unable to provide a dowry. However, the Prioress was concerned that she would be renouncing a successful public career. Father Provincial's approval had to be given before accepting her. Edith had to endure a further trial of patience before finally meeting their local Superior in place of the Provincial. No obstacles were put in her way and she was invited to meet the chapter nuns – that is the fully professed members of the community – in the parlour. As a special request she was asked to sing them a song, which she says was a worse ordeal than speaking to an audience of a thousand people! She cannot have performed too badly for the community voted to accept her.

Before leaving Münster, Edith wrote to Hatti: 'Now I'll tell you what is going to become of your godchild . . . On 14 July I will go from here to Cologne, at first as guest of the Carmelite Nuns . . . From mid-August until mid-October I want to go to my mother's, to prepare her gradually . . . I am going to enter as a postulant on 15 October . . . And you will help me, won't you, with your prayers during the difficult months in Breslau?'

Edith arrived in time to share the feast of Our Lady of Mount Carmel with the community. She stayed in the guesthouse outside the enclosure and joined them in chapel for their daily offices. She had the opportunity to meet with the sisters in their free time to learn more about their life. During her month at Carmel, she had the joy of completing Hedwig's

---

[1]This is Renata Posselt, Edith's first biographer. References to this work are from now on indicated in footnotes as Sister Teresia de Spiritu Sancto (name as stated on the English edition).

instruction and standing as sponsor at her baptism in the Cathedral Chapter-House. It was also a period of prayerful preparation for the task ahead of her – that of inflicting a second painful blow on the mother she loved so well.

When Edith arrived at Breslau railway station, she was happy to be met by Rosa in whom she was able to confide her future plans knowing that she was the one member of the family likely to understand her reasons for the commitment she was to make. During her first weeks at home, discussion about her future with her mother was avoided. Eventually it had to be faced. Across the decades and the miles, I can feel the pain both mother and daughter suffered as they did so. Many a good Catholic mother has endured anguish at the prospect of a daughter leaving home for ever to lead the cloistered life of a contemplative nun. How much greater the anguish of a mother whose very being and strong Jewish faith rejected Christianity. And who had so many misconceptions of the Catholic faith and the life her favourite daughter had chosen. All Edith's attempts at calming her fears were in vain. She realized she 'had to take the step entirely in the darkness of faith'.[2] She often wondered which of them would break first, but they both held until the last day.

The 'last' day was Edith's forty-second birthday and the Jewish Feast – not of the Atonement that year for it is a movable feast – but of the Tabernacles. Edith went to the synagogue with her mother in the morning and they prayed side by side. Afterwards, Auguste insisted on walking the three-quarters of a mile home in spite of her eighty-four years. Each last moment alone together was precious. Family and friends called later in the day to say their farewells. It was not until they were finally alone in the evening that the old lady expressed her grief with inconsolable tears. Edith comforted her as best she could, taking her upstairs and helping her to undress before putting her to bed. There was little sleep for either of them that night. Else and Rosa went with her to the station next morning. As she took her seat in the compartment after the last wave, she 'was in deep peace – in the haven of the Divine Will.'[3]

---

[2]Sister Teresia de Spiritu Sancto, p.128.
[3]ibid., p.131.

In a letter to Mother Petra written from Carmel three days later, she said: 'I saw only very great pain, in the face of which my leaving appeared to be an inconceivable cruelty.' After Vespers on 14 October, Edith arrived at the enclosure door: 'It opened at last, and in deep peace I stepped across the threshold into the House of the Lord.'[4]

However much Edith craved for Carmel, however great a woman of prayer she already was, those early weeks and months as a postulant and novice could not have been easy. She had always lived a well-disciplined life but by her own rule book. This included excesses of intellectual work, loss of sleep, irregular meals and, one might add, an overzealous prayer-life combined with strict fasting. In Carmel the days are tightly structured. The monastery bell is constantly ringing, calling the Sisters to prayer, to work, to meals, to recreation and to rest. In the summer months, the day at Cologne Carmel commenced at 4.30 a.m. and concluded after Matins and Lauds at around 10 p.m. It was a long day but Edith thrived on the regime and friends remarked on the new-found youth and joy which they found in her when they visited. She had to learn how to become a pupil again and how to share the novitiate with three others, all the best part of twenty years younger than herself. She had to learn to accept correction and leave her work immediately the bell went. She had to learn many small traditional and probably outdated Carmelite customs and submit happily to them. She had to forget the joy of the Benedictine liturgy and learn the Carmelite way of reciting the office in monotone. She had to learn to be an obedient humble child at the age of forty-two and at the height of her academic career. Formation years for a Carmelite are uncompromising and never easy. Abbot Raphael wrote: 'No one saw more clearly than she that as well as having to adjust herself to the poverty and simplicity emphasized there, she would also encounter much that would irritate her own cultured taste.'[5]

The Carmelite Rule became all important to her and she was an example to those in the novitiate in her observance of it. 'Day after day Sister Benedicta plunged ever more deeply into

---

[4]ibid., p.132.
[5]ibid., p.153.

the spirit of the Order in accordance with that counsel of the Foundress, which bids her daughters seek nothing but God alone and to give themselves unreservedly to His will.'[6]

Edith's clothing ceremony – the day on which she received her Carmelite habit – was arranged for 15 April 1934, significantly the feast of the Good Shepherd. Fifty years ago, the ceremony was rather different from that which is used today. As the bride of Christ, Edith wore a white wedding-dress and long white veil which was held in place by a myrtle wreath. The ceremony was charged with symbolism; the simpler one used today is less so. The chief celebrant at Edith's clothing Mass was, as it should be, Abbot Raphael. He was assisted by Father Provincial who clothed her and asked: 'What do you ask for?' Calmly and distinctly audible, Edith answered: 'The mercy of God, the poverty of the Order and the company of the sisters.'[7]

The Carmelite chapel had never before received so many bouquets of flowers or so many eminent guests. Friends from all Edith's former walks of life were present including 'dear Hatti'. A telegram was received from Husserl and greetings from all her religious friends who were unable to be present. Her one sadness was that no one from her own family was there. Rosa provided the white silk for the wedding-dress and Edith knew she was with her 'inwardly' all the way. Edith's choice of a name in religion, Sr Teresa Benedicta a Cruce, encapsulates so well the influences which had brought her to this clothing day. St Teresa had opened the door of truth, St Benedict had been responsible for much of her spiritual growth, and she held the Cross at the very centre of her life.

Before leaving Carmel on this historic day, Abbot Raphael had a few words in private with Edith when she was able to tell him 'that she was completely at home in heart and mind'.[8] They were never to meet again but kept in touch as long as it was possible so to do.

From this day on, Edith's Carmelite life followed the usual pattern. A year after her clothing, she made her First Profession of temporary vows. This is a private ceremony celebrated

[6]ibid., p.160.
[7]ibid., pp.145–146.
[8]ibid., p.154.

with her new family, the community. It was held on Easter Sunday morning at 6 o'clock, the time at which Prime and None were said. Edith wore a wreath of white roses and her vows were made in the hand of her Prioress. Her perpetual, solemn Profession followed three years later, on 21 April. The veiling ceremony, when her white veil was replaced by a black one, was on 1 May 1938, the Feast of the Good Shepherd . . . He had seen her safely to her chosen earthly home. She was now a full member of the Carmelite community.

Every Carmelite monastery is autonomous and each has its own charism, its own *horarium* (this varies only in the timetable and not the substance) and its own manner of work to earn a living. Cologne Carmel was in a unique situation early in the twentieth century.

There were no Carmelite friars in its region. In fact, the Provincial came from Belgium . . . no doubt the reason why Edith never met him! In the absence of friars, the Carmel found it had many external demands and was an important centre of Carmelite spirituality. From this centre there developed a Confraternity of the Scapular, a Third Order group (founded in 1916 and which had its own library at the Carmel), a Brotherhood of St Thérèse (canonically erected in 1928) and a Teresian prayer-group. The sisters had to respond to these external demands which required a deepening of their own Carmelite charism. Their apostolate was writing. In one of her letters, Edith writes: 'We do not have our own publishing house; but having three "authoresses" in the house means we are selling a good number of publications on commission.' Two members of the community were gifted translators from German into French, Dutch and Flemish. Another spoke English and was a gifted artist.

Mother Renata replaced Mother Josepha as Prioress in 1936. The former had entered Carmel at the age of twenty-eight after having studied music and domestic science in Bonn and Belgium and having run a youth group in Berlin. She had a mature experience of the world and was able to appreciate and empathize with her singular novice, Edith.

This then was the background to the Cologne Carmel which accepted the challenge of so unusual an aspirant as Edith. After her clothing, their newly appointed Provincial from Bavaria, Father Theodor Rauch, spent some time with Edith discussing her earlier philosophical work. It is likely he already knew something of her reputation. Before leaving, he instructed the Prioress to relieve her of all other duties so that she might continue her work. This did not set a precedent. Edith was subsequently expected to undertake many of the ordinary day-to-day tasks throughout her life in Carmel.

Edith had brought to Carmel her opus on *Potentiality and Act* and *Life in a Jewish Family*. She also had the index to her St Thomas translation to complete. There appear to have been two work periods in the Cologne timetable, one of two hours and another of one hour. It could not have been easy to undertake intellectual work of this order in such brief periods. *Life in a Jewish Family* acted as a relief from the intense concentration required for her more serious work. Edith wrote to a friend: 'The daily schedule of Carmel allows very little time for scholarly work. That I should be permitted such work while still in the novitiate is an exception.' We may be sure not everyone in the community approved of this exception being made! Many other demands ate into her work time. Sketches of St Teresa and St Margaret Redi who was canonized in the same year as Edith's clothing, various essays and meditations for special occasions, all were required of her in the normal course of events. Beyond this, she had to find time for letter-writing, usually at the end of the day between 8 and 9 p.m.

Quite soon after she entered, the following was her answer to a friend's enquiry: 'I have never been forbidden to write to you. But I have been given the general directive to limit myself to what is most necessary.' How difficult this must have been for one with so many friendships. As I thumb my way through the one hundred and ninety-six letters written and published between October 1933 and August 1942, it is easy to recognize her loyalty to those who had come to depend on her wise advice. It is also apparent, to me at least, that Edith in her own turn very much relied on the continued friendship and contact with Hatti and Mother Petra. Hatti was a faithful friend with whom Edith could share her intellectual work, occasionally seeking her opinion and encouragement. A visit to Cologne from Hatti would, Edith exclaimed, 'be a gift from heaven'. While with Mother Petra, it was her religious life and family concerns that she shared.

Edith's letters to Mother Petra show a greater warmth and affection than those written to anyone else. I have puzzled over this relationship and wonder how it became so deep after one brief stay at Dorsten and very few subsequent meetings. 'Vulnerable' is not a term one readily associates with Edith. However, a religious superior such as Mother Petra, who was twelve years older than Edith, would be more alive than most to the agony of a daughter parting with a mother in Edith's unusual circumstances. Did she discover in Edith one who was in need of a 'surrogate' mother who could sustain her with love and understanding through the parting and the entry to Carmel? Edith once wrote: 'Now I always have the feeling that you are doing for me what my own mother would do, had she an understanding of our life.' This, I believe, is exactly how it was.

When Edith entered Carmel, Mother Petra's first gift was a breviary, the daily office of the Church in three volumes, essential to the monastic way of life. She regularly sent gifts, not alone for Edith but for those in the novitiate with her, an Easter Candle and an Easter rabbit for each of them on one occasion. On another, something 'extra' the entire community could share. Above all, Edith thanked her for her love which she said she had in no way earned. They constantly communed in prayer, in a special way for Edith's important ceremonies and for Carmelite and Ursuline related feasts. Edith writes of waiting for a whole year for a visit from Mother Petra and we can assume she made more than one to Cologne Carmel.

After Auguste Stein's death, Mother Petra visited Breslau and met her sisters Frieda and Rosa, and Edith realized she was going in her place. Moreover, Edith placed a protégée of hers, Ruth Kantorowicz, in her care when she entered Carmel. Edith returned Mother Petra's kindness in her own way in her deep prayer life and with her small personal gifts such as it was possible to send from Carmel, one of her own essays or meditations maybe. The trust between them was implicit.

In December 1939, Edith wrote a beautiful dialogue between Mother Ursula – almost certainly with Mother Petra in mind – and Sister Angela, the foundress of the Ursuline Order.[9] This shows how well Edith understood Mother Petra's

---

[9] 'I Am Always in Your Midst', in Edith Stein, *The Hidden Life*, pp.116–121.

concerns and responsibilities at Dorsten. She 'took' them with her to Echt and the bonds of prayer remained ever strong.

In her biography, Mother Renata writes: 'As a Carmelite Sister Benedicta did not close her heart to all those whom she had loved in the world ... Edith used to watch over her friends' lives with affectionate concern.'[10] Yes, the concerns of her friends remained in her constant care. One who was in need of more than most was Ruth Kantorowicz.

Ruth, who was Edith's junior by ten years, lived in Hamburg and was a friend of her sister Else and her family. I can only surmise that her first letter to Edith (received shortly before she entered Carmel) concerned uncertainty about her future. Ruth was a Jew on the way to conversion and in need of guidance and moral support. When Edith places her in Mother Petra's care, she refers to her as 'the poor protégé'. Ruth was received into the Church in 1934. She approached Edith again with queries about the religious life and her own leanings in this direction. Edith strongly advised patience but offered any practical help she was able to give. Ruth was invited to spend her first Christmas as a Christian at Cologne Carmel and to spend some time discussing her future with Edith. She returned again in April and by the autumn decided she would be happier living in Cologne. She did so existing on occasional work, some of which was supplied by Edith. Her last published letter to Ruth is a covering note regarding the manuscripts she was sending her to be typed. Edith, together with her community, was very supportive of Ruth but they felt unable to accept her as a postulant owing to the worsening political situation.

In August 1936, Ruth entered the Maastricht Carmel in Holland. After ten months as a postulant she was rejected for entry to the novitiate. This was against the wish of her Prioress and novice mistress but the community vote was the deciding factor. This was a cruel blow to Ruth.

By this time, there was no question of a non-Aryan returning to Germany. The Ursuline sisters of Venlo offered her sanctuary in their extern quarters where she was a 'maid for all jobs'. Do we see Mother Petra's hand in this act of charity from the Ursulines?

---

[10]Sister Teresia de Spiritu Sancto, pp.157–158.

There are no further letters published from Edith to Ruth but a mutual friend, Hedwig Dülberg, received urgent entreaties from Edith to visit Ruth in Holland. The lives of Edith and Ruth came together again when Edith arrived in Holland and Ruth continued her work on Edith's manuscripts. There is nothing to suggest they met again until their last journey in the SS cattle trucks.

A fitting conclusion to this piece on Ruth is a footnote to Letter 211 in *Self-Portrait in Letters*: 'Ruth Kantorowicz continued to type, in grateful love, with extraordinary understanding, thousands of pages of manuscript for Edith Stein to the very last days. She was familiar with Edith Stein's handwriting and the often unclear phrasing of the text because of insertions, footnotes, etc. Beyond the grave that has no gravestone, the thanks of all of us go out to Ruth Kantorowicz, this quiet, frail, highly gifted friend of Edith Stein's.'

Needless to say, friendships were not a distraction to everyday Carmelite life. Edith soon discovered how inadequate she was at the daily household chores and her attempts at simple needlework had to be unpicked and redone. Humiliations such as this had to be endured. But the community soon discovered she could do more than write when she asked permission to nurse Sister Clara, a lay sister who was dying of cancer. She did this with great devotion for three and a half months before being transferred to the task of portress (turn sister). This is a responsible post and it is unusual for a sister to be assigned to such a position of trust before final vows.

Feast days and Holy days in Carmel are celebrated with a dispensation from work, and entertainments are arranged – concerts, one-act plays, skits and puppet-shows. These are prepared by a few for the benefit of the rest. Edith was invariably involved, either writing the text or performing a part. On one occasion, she played St Francis. On another, the Voice of God. On Holy Innocents Day, the novices were in charge. Edith had recently returned from hospital with her leg in plaster. She was placed, well hidden in the wings, and as St Gabriel, the Angel of the Incarnation, walked onto the stage, Edith's Voice of God rang out with great majesty. She always joined in with lively enthusiasm, always ready for a good laugh. She once said she had never laughed as much as she did in Carmel. It is amazing what a well stocked dressing-up cupboard and good simple fun can generate in the way of laughter! Edith had no difficulty settling into the life of the conventual family, making friends with each one and feeling at ease among them.

Edith made a simple request when she entered Carmel – that she might continue her long-held habit of writing a weekly letter to her mother. This was granted. For many months she received no reply but Rosa's regular letter was eagerly awaited. The Carmelite Sisters at the foundation in Breslau became Auguste's faithful friends. One day, unbeknown to Rosa or anyone else, she had made a visit to the building-site of the new monastery. After this visit, she began to include a few lines at the foot of Rosa's letter. The wounds were beginning to heal but were cruelly reopened when Auguste was found to be suffering from terminal cancer. She could not understand why Edith was unable to visit her and felt that her youngest daughter had forsaken her. It was a heart-wrenching situation for them both.

Auguste died on 14 September 1936 at the same time as the sisters in Cologne Carmel were renewing their vows. This was customary on the Feast of the Exaltation of the Cross each year. As Edith stood in choir waiting her turn, she had a strong feeling of her mother's presence at her side. It was the precise moment at which Auguste left this world for the next. While Edith mourned, she was grateful that her mother should be relieved of further suffering. Mother Renata gave her permission to dig some snowdrops from the monastery garden which were sent to Rosa for her mother's grave as a '*living greeting*'.[11] She wrote to Sr Callista: 'My mother held to her faith to the very last. The faith and firm confidence she had in her God from her earliest childhood . . . stayed alive in her during the final difficult agony. Therefore, I have the firm belief that she found a very merciful judge and is now my most faithful helper on my way.'

In her will, Auguste left 38 Michaelisstrasse in the care of Frieda and Rosa, with the request that they would maintain it as a permanent home for the rest of the family as she had

---

[11]Romaeus Leuven, OCD, *Heil im Unheil. Das Leben Edith Steins, Reife und Vollendung*, Druten: 'De Maas & Waler" & Freiburg, Basel & Vienna, Herder (*Edith Steins Werke*, X), 1983, p.123.

always done. But this was not to be for long. This close-knit, honest, God-fearing family could not escape the persecution of the Jews. Some of them fled to America, others perished in a concentration camp.

After her mother's death, it was arranged that Rosa should visit Cologne from 16–29 December, to be reunited with Edith and receive her final instruction before her reception into the Church. By an extraordinary act of God's providence, Edith was able to share this special occasion with her. A few days earlier, Edith had fallen and broken her left wrist and ankle. Rosa's baptism took place in the hospital church at Hohenlind on 24 December at 4 p.m. Edith was given permission to attend before returning home to Carmel. At Midnight Mass, Rosa made her First Holy Communion. How richly she was rewarded for her steadfastness! Edith wrote a beautiful poem on Rosa's behalf in memory of the happy occasion. It was my introduction to Edith Stein and so has to be included here.

Holy Night

In Remembrance of Christmas Eve 1936[12]

My Lord and God,
You have guided me on a long, dark road,
Stony and hard.
How often the strength has gone from me,
And I almost hoped never to see the light.
Yet when my heart sickened in the depths of sorrow
A star rose before me, gentle and clear.
Steadily it guided me – and I followed.
Stumbling at first, but ever more surely.
Until at last I stood before the door of the Church.
It was opened – I prayed to enter –
And from the lips of your priest I received your blessing.
Within shone row upon row of stars,
Red Christmas stars,[13] showing me the way to you.
They led me forward.
The secret of my heart, which for so long I had to hide,

---

[12]This poem is given as reproduced in Sister Teresia de Spiritu Sancto, pp.171–172.
[13]The Church of Hohenlind was brightly decorated with flowers known as 'Christmas Stars'.

I now proclaim aloud
I believe, I confess!
The priest takes me with him up the altar steps,
I bow my head –
And the holy water cleanses my soul.
Is it possible, Lord, to be born again
After leaving a mother's womb?
It is You who said it and You I believe.
The burden and sorrow of a life-time fell from me.
Standing up I received the white cloak[14]
That was laid on my shoulders,
The shining symbol of purity!
I carried a candle in my hand,
Its flame announcing the glow of your holiness within me.
Now my heart has become a crib
Waiting for your Son.
Though not for long!
Mary, my Mother and your Mother,
Has given me her name
And at midnight gives me her newly born Child
To lay in my heart.
No human heart could ever conceive
What you are preparing for those who love you.
Now I possess you and will never leave you.
For wherever the road of life leads me, you are beside me,
Nothing can ever divide me from your love.

Rosa returned to Breslau where she was confirmed on Pentecost Sunday. For the time being, she lived peaceably at the family home.

The foundation stone of the Breslau Carmel was laid in July 1935 but it had to suffer many tribulations in the following years. In 1945 the new monastery – from which the Sisters had fled earlier – was burnt to the ground. Attempts to settle elsewhere in the neighbourhood failed. Finally, in 1953 they transferred to Witten-on-the-Ruhr where a Carmel survives to this day.

Edith knew only too well that the peace and security which she found in Cologne Carmel was not unlimited. On 10 April 1938, before her final profession, the polling officers arrived without any warning, asking for the Sisters' vote. It was the

---

[14]The white cloak was Edith's Carmelite mantle.

day of Hitler's plebiscite. As they called the register and came
to Stein, they were told: 'She has not the right . . . She is a
non-Aryan';[15] this was noted on the register. The *Kristall-
nacht* followed on 9 November, the pogroms broke out across
Germany and the Cologne synagogue was burnt to the ground.
Edith's premonition that Christ's Cross would be laid on the
Jewish people became a stark reality. She feared for the safety
of her community if she remained in their midst. Letters were
written first to Palestine and then to Holland to see if the
Carmel in Bethlehem or Echt would accept her. The former
was unable to do so (Palestine had refused to allow any more
German Jews to immigrate) but Echt – originally a foundation
from Cologne – offered her a welcome. Throughout Advent
1938, plans were made for her departure with, at Edith's
request, a minimum of fuss. On a foggy night, 31 December,
Dr Paul Strerath and his companion, Dr Leo Sudbrack, drove
her across the border.

Before we follow Edith to Echt, it is timely to reflect on her
five years in Carmel and the changes they had wrought in her.
In 1932, Daniel Feuling OSB had met Edith at the Juvisy
Conference where her erudite contribution to the discussion
left a lasting impression on him. He met her again some time
later in Carmel and in 1956 he wrote a short biographical
sketch. A quotation is worthy of inclusion: 'In her *spiritual-
religious security*, I sensed a greater maturity in Sr Benedicta.
Formerly she had been engaged in a struggle of the mind, . . .
striving for clarity of knowledge and a firm basis for cogni-
tion. But now she had entered into a new way of living the
truth . . . She had reached the other shore.'[16] This is a
profound statement and bears witness to Edith's conviction
that the Lord held something special for her in Carmel. Here
she attained tranquillity of mind and heart. She was well
prepared for what lay ahead of her.

*

1 January 1939 was the seventeenth anniversary of Edith's
baptism and reception into the Church. She found herself cele-

---

[15]Sister Teresia de Spiritu Sancto, p.183.
[16]Daniel Feuling, OSB, 'Short Biographical Sketch of Edith Stein', in Waltraud Herbstrith, OCD (ed.), op.cit., (pp.260–263), p.262.

brating in a strange land in a new community, far from her blood family, friends and her much-loved Cologne sisters. The Echt community gave Edith the warmest of welcomes and never failed in their kindness. She repeatedly expressed her gratitude for this. But it did not take away her pain, and in a letter to Mother Petra she says no human words can provide consolation: only 'he who lays the cross [on us] understands well how to make the burden light and sweet.'

On 1 January, the Prioress took Edith to visit the graves of the Cologne foundation Sisters. They too had been driven from their homeland and here she found some comfort in the link they provided with her own dear community.

Edith determined to learn Dutch, no great difficulty for her. Rather more difficult was learning to adapt where 'everything here is all new again'. The Sisters soon recognized her zeal, her simplicity and her warmth. They noticed the great weight of sadness which she carried but also her willingness to join in a joke and have a good laugh. There were times when she displayed disapproval at the noisiness of one Sister and the lack of attention to duty of another. She did so without using words!

It was never easy to transfer from one Carmel to another and the disposition of the house at Echt could hardly have been more different from that of Cologne. The Sisters earned their livelihood by carrying out simple sewing tasks and embroidery and undertaking washing for the parish and the Abbey, work at which Edith knew only too well she was inadequate. There were eighteen Sisters in community, four of whom were seventy years or older and three of whom were lay Sisters. A new foundation in 1938 in Beek had undoubtedly absorbed some of the stronger members of the community.

In October, Edith wrote to Sr Agnella: 'Since the middle of June, I've been second portress and have charge of the refectory. Added to that are common labours in this large, rural household (big laundry days, harvesting fruit – an overabundance of it this year – and preserving it, cleaning the house, etc.). After our seven hours of prayer, then, there is little time left to spend at the desk.' Earlier letters imply that during her first months in Echt she was allowed time to settle in. She had brought the galleys of her big opus with her, *Finite and Eternal Being* (in its embryo this was *Potentiality and Act*), and she was allowed to spend time proof-reading it and preparing the index. It was in the hands of publisher Otto Borgmeyer who later had to withdraw because Edith's name as a Jew was not on the register of the State Chamber of Literature. Edith was disheartened by this and the index was never completed. She considered this work her farewell gift to Germany and it was a sadness for her not to see it published. This is not surprising when one realizes that she began her work on *Potentiality and Act* during her time at Speyer. It was conceived as a thesis for *Habilitation* when she decided to try again for a university post. She was working on it during the months at home (1931–1932) and also on and off while at Münster. It was only thanks to the foresight of Father Provincial Rauch, who instructed Cologne's Prioress to allow Edith time to continue this work, that it was completed. We know that she then gave the work its new title, *Finite and Eternal Being*, and that she rewrote most of it. This, her major work, was in the making over a period of six years and was finally published in 1950. An interesting footnote to this is a little treatise, an appendix to the main work, which Edith wrote while in Cologne Carmel in 1936: *Seelenburg*, the 'Castle of the Soul', was published independently of the main work twelve years later in 1962.

Edith did not attempt to take the manuscript of *Life in a Jewish Family* across the border, realizing her luggage would be searched. In February 1939, she made cautious enquiries in Cologne about the possibility of having the manuscript brought to Echt. A young Marianhill missionary, Dr Rhabanus Laubenthal, undertook the task of bringing it. Providentially, the customs officers gave the manuscript a cursory glance and decided it was his thesis! On 7 January she had written: 'Today, finally, after many wondrous developments, it is possible for me to resume [these notes] once more.' All too few further pages were completed. They covered her weeks in Freiburg preparing for and achieving her doctorate. It is possible that returning to this work was a form of therapy in this desolate period of her life.

When the Germans invaded Holland in May 1940, a safe place had to be found for the manuscript. Sr Pia, first portress and her good friend, helped her wrap it carefully before burying it in the monastery graveyard. After three months,

Edith decided to retrieve it, for what reason no one knows. Having done so, she left it in Sr Pia's care as if she could no longer decide for herself what best to do with it. Sr Pia chose a safe corner in the cellar where it remained until the end of the war. As the situation in Holland worsened, the Sisters had to abandon their monastery and it lay empty. After the war, when Sr Pia learned the building was to be requisitioned, she returned to Echt to recover the manuscript which happily she found where she had hidden it. She passed it onto the Discalced Father Provincial. *Life in a Jewish Family* has been the bedrock, the source from which Edith's life has surged and spread with such vitality. Would we have known Edith in the way we do without this personal introduction to her?

On Passion Sunday, 26 March 1939, Edith wrote to her Prioress, Mother Ottilia, asking to be allowed to 'offer myself to the heart of Jesus as a sacrifice of propitiation for true peace, that the dominion of the Antichrist may collapse . . . I would like it [my request] granted this very day because it is the twelfth hour.' This gives us some idea of her inner suffering.

Edith's letters to Mother Petra and Sr Agnella express growing concerns for her family, especially Rosa who was having difficulty getting out of Germany. Eventually she does so, but Rosa's journey continues to be 'stony and hard'. She answered an advertisement from Belgium where recruits for a new foundation of Sisters were being invited. Her confidence in the correspondence between them was misplaced and she lost the few possessions she was able to bring out of Germany. She arrived at Echt with little but the clothes she was wearing. The community extended their kindness to Rosa and she was given a room in the extern quarters where she was able to assist Paula who cared for the Sisters' needs outside. When Rosa received her resident's permit in Holland, she hoped to be accepted for the novitiate as an extern Sister but the Echt community felt the time was not suitable. Instead she was encouraged to become a tertiary member of the Order. She and Edith met once a week for her to receive instruction and this gave them the opportunity to come together in their 'aloneness'. Rosa was received in June 1940 and professed the following year when she took the name Sister Rosa Maria of Jesus. In June 1941, when Paula retired, Rosa took her place as housekeeper and sacristan, a task which gave her great joy.

Edith's faithful friends, Hatti and Mother Petra, each visited her on at least one occasion. She confided in Hatti how difficult it was to get used to the little details of daily life. And she writes rather a sad letter to Mother Petra after her visit in 1940: 'I was still somewhat depressed because, when you were kind enough to visit me, I was unable to spend as much time with you as you had set aside to give me . . . Surely you understood readily that, even to honour the dearest guest, I did not want to be absent for too long from our communal work. As it is, I am all too weak a member of the work force for all we have to do here in the house.' It is apparent from further letters that she was feeling very isolated from friends and family. After the German invasion, letter-writing was much reduced. I notice she was still in touch with Abbot Raphael who was living the life of a simple monk in Algeria, and with Ruth Kantorowicz who was busy typing a minor work of Edith's for a periodical in the USA.

Edith continued to appreciate the difficulties of others, no matter how intense her own. A typical example is her concern for the lay Sisters. She wrote to Mother Petra and Sr Agnella for the guidelines laid down by their Orders (Ursuline and Dominican) for auxiliary or lay Sisters. She was interested in their formation, prayer-life and work duties. She wanted to write something to cover this 'grey area' in the Carmelite life. As so often, Edith was way ahead of her time with this questioning.

A letter written to her brother-in-law, Hans Biberstein (Erna's husband), on the occasion of his fiftieth birthday betrays a little of Edith which we rarely penetrate: a hint of sentimentality, of nostalgia for days past and a yearning for news of the family closest to her heart who by this time were far away in the USA. She writes: 'What a celebration that would have been in Breslau! . . . The two of us[17] will spend the day with you in spirit . . . You will surely recall the time of your engagement . . . our walks together from the *Stadt-graben* (where I was then staying with Aunt Bianca) to Max Street or from there to Michaelis Street. It is amazing how long ago all that happened . . . I wonder: will we live to see the events of our days become "history"? . . . Perhaps these

---

[17]Edith and Rosa.

aphorisms may spur you on to let me in on some of your own thoughts. I would be happy, but if you cannot find the time I understand.' How could Hans ignore this gentle plea? More than a year later, Edith wrote to Mother Petra with news of the progress of the Biberstein children who were doing well at college – news sent to her by Hans.

Two years later, on 12 October 1941, Edith was celebrating her own fiftieth birthday. The community ensured it was a day of celebration and, knowing Edith's love of the Old Testament, they brought together an assembly of ten noble Patriarchs and Prophets from Abraham to Moses and Elisha as described in Ecclesiasticus 44–48. No doubt they had recourse to their dressing-up cupboard. Abraham was a most distinguished person played by Mother Subprioress. While Moses was small and quaint apart from his impressive nose. Last week's kitchen list was poorly concealed on the reverse side of his Tablet of Commandments. I wonder how Noah was portrayed and whether Elijah was waving a torch? I can image the peals of laughter from the audience and the lack of serious faces from the performers! Edith's letter to a friend tell us that it had only been possible for the community to put on such a large production thanks to the addition of five new postulants. An incredible blessing for a Carmel in such hard times and a pleasure for Edith to be asked to coach them with their Latin.

In November 1940, Edith wrote to Hatti to say that a new Prioress, Mother Antonia, had recently been elected and would like her to write something again. Later the same month, she wrote to Mother Johanna, Prioress of Beek, to say she was gathering material for a new work and that she was grateful to be allowed once more to do something 'before my brain rusts completely'. The new work was her last, *The Science of the Cross*, which she was preparing for the four hundredth anniversary of the birth of St John of the Cross on 24 June 1942. She became totally immersed in this work which was, as it were, a race against time and circumstance. It was written as she learned of the internment of three members of her family in Germany and as she endeavoured to make plans for Rosa and herself to leave Holland before it was too late. It was published as 'unfinished' but today it is understood to have been completed by her own death. Several of Edith's last published letters are written to the Prioress of

Beek Carmel asking for books to assist her with this work. *The Science of the Cross* is an in-depth study of the themes used by St John of the Cross in his mystical works. In Edith's analysis, the Doctrine of the Cross lies at their core. While this work is undoubtedly Edith's main mystical work, authorities no longer consider it to be a major work on John of the Cross. It is suggested that she wrote it for the benefit of her Carmelite sisters rather than for learned theologians. It was published in 1950, and a current English translation by Sr Josephine Koeppel is eagerly awaited.

On 9 June 1939, Edith had made her last will and testament: the arrangements for the posthumous publication of *Finite and Eternal Being* to be left to Father Provincial; her books to be donated to the Carmel with the exception of some academic volumes which the Trappist or Jesuit Fathers might value; two manuscripts to be returned to their respective owners, Dr Bell and Dr Ingarden; *Life in a Jewish Family* not to be published while her brothers and sisters were still alive and only thereafter if the Order thought fit. She added: 'I already now joyfully accept the death for which God has destined me, in complete submission to His Most Holy Will.'[18]

---

[18]Translated from: Leuven, op.cit., p.148.

CHAPTER TEN

Completion

At five o'clock on the evening of 2 August 1942, the Carmelite community of Echt were in chapel for their customary hour of meditation. The theme was being read by Sister Teresa Benedicta. Their meditation was rudely interrupted by the arrival of two SS officers who demanded that Sister Stein leave the convent with them in five minutes. As Mother Antonia and Edith remonstrated, they extended it to ten minutes but no more. Edith was ordered to bring with her a blanket, a mug, a spoon and three days' rations. The Sisters quickly helped her gather a few things together. What, I wonder, was happening to poor Rosa who also had to leave in ten minutes? After receiving the blessing of the Prioress, Edith turned to Rosa and said: 'Come, let us go for our people.' The two of them were driven away in a police van and nobody knew where to.

The preceding months had been anxious times for the Stein sisters. They had travelled to Maastricht and to Amsterdam in order to comply with orders to report for emigration. Positive efforts were made for them to leave Holland and a welcome had been received from Le Pâquier Carmel in Switzerland. But the necessary emigration papers, visas and entry permits were held up by excessive red tape. A pastoral letter was read in all Catholic churches on Sunday 26 July in which the Bishops expressed concern at the distress of Jews who were being deported to work abroad. The pastoral letter aroused tension in Holland and the people were fearful of its consequences. On Sunday 2 August, a week later, all non-Aryan members of every Dutch religious community were arrested as a reprisal to the Bishops' pastoral letter.

The police van took Edith and Rosa to Roermond where, together with twenty-eight others, they were driven in two vans to the transit camp of Amersfoort. The drivers lost their way in the dark and they did not arrive until three o'clock in the morning. They were shown to a hut which contained bunk beds but were given nothing to eat. After little sleep, they endured a long day at Amersfoort where the treatment was rough and repeated roll calls were taken. During the course of the following night, they were herded into freight trains which took them to the railway station of Hooghalen. From there they had to walk five kilometres across rough open land to the camp of Westerbork. Prior to 1939, Westerbork was a camp for refugees but following the German occupation, it became a concentration camp. It housed many Jews and not all were in transit as were Edith and her companions. It was run under a heartless and manipulative regime where husbands were separated from their wives and children, where those with artistic talents were forced to entertain the Commandant and his men. Many of the mothers were in a state of despair and their children neglected. During the three days they spent in the camp, Edith was able to comfort and assist them and was remembered for this by those who survived. It was possible, with the assistance of the Red Cross, to send messages to Echt. In her first note from Barracks 36, it is apparent Edith held some hope of release. She enclosed a note for the Swiss Consulate in Amsterdam asking for permission to cross the border. She asked Mother Antonia to send their ID and ration cards and said there was no need to worry about them: 'We are very calm and cheerful.' They had met Ruth and further members of religious orders and were praying together. In her second note, Edith tells Mother Antonia that the manuscript on *The Science of the Cross* is at Venlo (to be typed by Ruth) and asks her to send for it. Did Edith consider this to be her parting gift to the community of Echt? Her second request was for their prayers on which she said they all counted. Her final note, written on 6 August, mentions that a transport was leaving early next day. For Silesia or Czechoslovakia? Did she expect to be on this? She asks for some essentials. For Rosa, warm clothing, a toothbrush, a cross and a rosary and for herself, the next volume of the breviary. She adds: 'so far I have been able to pray gloriously.' My intuition that Rosa may have been panic-stricken and unable to pack for herself when the SS arrived was justified by these requests. In the evening of the same day, 6 August, messengers arrived from Echt for Edith and Rosa and from Venlo for Ruth, with luggage to supply some of their urgent needs. These good men had a difficult journey to Westerbork and were pleased to be able to speak with the sisters at the entrance to the camp and to exchange news before handing over the bags. On their return to Echt, one of them reported on Edith's demeanour, saying: 'Calmly and in complete surrender she had placed her life into the sure hand of God.'[1] She was still wearing the habit with the yellow star attached and was anxious to know if Mother had sent her a replacement habit as she intended to continue wearing one.

Edith's short notes (described as telegrams) to Mother Antonia, express no emotion or complaint and deal only with practical matters. There is no mention of stress or anxiety. A few simple lines from Rosa to Mother are more revealing: 'We have slept very little, but have had a lot of good air and much travelling.' Dear Rosa, how grateful she must have been for Edith's quiet courage.

Schifferstadt was a railway station well known to Edith. It was convenient for Speyer and was the home town of the Schwind family. At midday on 7 August, Valentin Fouquet, the station-master at Schifferstadt, was on duty. He was a well-respected man and easily recognized by the red cap which he never failed to wear. He was expecting train D5, the express from Saarbrücken to Ludwigshafen. As it drew into platform 3, he could see that extra sealed carriages had been coupled to the train. They were windowless freight trucks with only a narrow slit for ventilation and were transporting Jewish prisoners. When Edith was aware that they were entering Schifferstadt, she moved towards the slit and asked Valentin Fouquet if he knew the Schwind family. When he replied in the affirmative, she asked him to pass on greetings from Edith Stein and to say

---

[1]P.O. van Kempen, 'Eyewitness in Westerbork', in Waltraud Herbstrith, OCD (ed.), op.cit. (pp.272–276), pp.274–275.

she was travelling east. Valentin remembered her as the lady in dark clothes. Edith then noticed a priest standing on the platform. It was Ferdinand Meckes, a curate from Ludwigshafen. She asked him to pass on her good wishes to her former colleagues at Speyer. He saw a pair of eyes – Edith's eyes – through the chink in the truck which was festooned with barbed wire. As the train drew out of the station, a note dropped through the chink and was later recovered from the railway line by the priest. On it was written: '*Unterwegs ad orientem*' (on the way to the east) and it was signed: 'Sister Teresa Benedicta a Cruce'. It was subsequently delivered to her friend at St Lioba, Sister Placida, who burned it before her own arrest some time later.

The train remained in the station for a total of only ten to fifteen minutes. This was the last sighting of Edith Stein, and her death in Auschwitz on 9 August was not verified by the Red Cross until February 1950. Today, a memorial plaque in Edith's honour hangs between platforms 3 and 2 at Schifferstadt station.

Inevitably there remain so many unanswered questions. Edith and Rosa were two of nine hundred and eighty-five prisoners transported that day from Westerbork to Auschwitz. Did they all go to the gas chamber on arrival at the camp? If so, why? Was it not the policy of the SS to retain all but the old and sick for work in the mines and elsewhere? Did the Commandant know who the Carmelite nun was and if so, was Dr Edith Stein more likely to meet her end quickly? The length of the journey must have been unendurable for so large a number of prisoners in sealed compartments. Had their route been the direct one via north Germany rather than the one taken through Luxembourg, central Germany and Czechoslovakia, it would surely have reduced their travel time by more than half. One can imagine the pitiable state of the prisoners when they finally left the wagons.

As I have endeavoured to follow these last days of Edith's life, I realize that hitherto I have shielded myself from the reality of what her dying in Auschwitz truly meant. Books and films have portrayed the stark facts but somehow the people you know are never there, they have not endured the humiliation of stripping, disinfecting and gassing. It would be just too awful to contemplate. Here and now, I find myself face to face with those facts. Yes, Edith and Rosa did share this terrible fate with hundreds and thousands of others. After cremation, their ashes were sprinkled on the River Sola and flowed downstream. The last vestige of their lives disappeared.

Controversy over Edith's canonization can take nothing away from her person or her life. She had surely earned the jewels in the crown of martyrdom long before she reached Auschwitz; in her painful pilgrimage of search for the truth and in her total dedication to that truth, whatever the sacrifices, until those final awful days. Hers was a life of fidelity to family, friends, scholarship, Carmel and ultimately, to her God, revealed to her in the Cross of life, the Cross on which her Saviour died, *he* who became the well-spring of her very being.

Select Bibliography

The main works consulted on Edith Stein are:

Batzdorff, Susanne M., *Aunt Edith. The Jewish Heritage of a Catholic Saint*, Springfield, Illinois, Templegate, 1998.

Fabrégues, Jean de, *Edith Stein. Philosopher, Carmelite Nun, Holocaust Martyr*, Boston, MA, St Paul Books and Media, 1993.

Feldes, Joachim, *Edith Stein und Schifferstadt*, Schifferstadt, Geier-Druck-Verlag, 1998.

Fermín, Francisco Javier Sancho, OCD, *Edith Stein. Modelo y Maestra de Espiritualidad en la Escuela del Carmelo Teresiano*, 2nd ed., Burgos, Editorial Monte Carmelo (Estudios Monte Carmelo, 18), 1998.

Graef, Hilda, C., *The Scholar and the Cross. The Life and Work of Edith Stein,* London, New York & Toronto, Longmans, 1955.

Herbstrith, Waltraud, OCD (ed.), *Never Forget. Christian and Jewish Perspectives on Edith Stein*, tr Susanne Batzdorff, Washington, ICS Publications, 1998.

Herrmann, Maria Adele, OP, *Die Speyerer Jahre von Edith Stein. Aufzeichnungen zu ihrem 100. Geburtstag,* Speyer, Pilger-Verlag, 1990.

Koeppel, Josephine, OCD, *Edith Stein. Philosopher and Mystic,* Collegeville, Minnesota, The Liturgical Press, 1990.

Leuven, Romaeus, OCD, *Heil im Unheil. Das Leben Edith Steins: Reife und Vollendung,* Druten, 'De Maas & Waler' & Freiburg, Basel & Vienna, Herder (*Edith Steins Werke, X*), 1983.

Neyer, Amata, ODC, *Edith Stein. A Saint for Our Times,* tr Sr Lucia Wiedenhöver, ODC, Darlington Carmel, c. 1975.

Oben, Freda Mary, *Edith Stein. Scholar, Feminist, Saint,* New York, Alba House (Society of St Paul), 1988.

—, 'Edith Stein the Woman', in John Sullivan, OCD (ed.), *Carmelite Studies,* IV *(Edith Stein Symposium, Teresian Culture),* Washington, ICS Publications, 1987, pp.3–33.

[Posselt], Sister Teresia [Renata] de Spiritu Sancto, ODC, *Edith Stein,* trs Cecily Hastings and Donald Nicholl, London & New York, Sheed and Ward, 1952.